Online Trading for Beginners

Learn the Basics of Technical Analysis and Build Your Path to Financial Independence

Max Fortune

Copyright © 2025 – Max Fortune

All Rights Reserved.

This document is designed to provide accurate and reliable information regarding the subject matter and topics discussed. The publication is sold with the understanding that the publisher is not obligated to provide accounting, legally authorized, or otherwise qualified services. If legal or professional advice is required, the services of a practicing professional should be sought.

It is strictly prohibited to reproduce, duplicate, or transmit any part of this document in electronic or printed format. Recording this publication is strictly forbidden, as is storing this document without prior written consent from the publisher. All rights reserved.

The information provided in this document is stated to be truthful and consistent. Any liability arising from the use or misuse of the policies, processes, or directions contained herein rests solely and entirely with the reader. Under no circumstances will the publisher be held liable for any damages, losses, or monetary expenses resulting from the information contained herein, whether directly or indirectly.

The information contained in this document is provided solely for informational purposes and is universal in nature. The presentation of such information is without contract or any form of guarantee. Trademarks used within this book are included solely for clarification purposes and remain the property of their respective owners, who are not affiliated with this document.

Sommario

Introduction 8

Chapter 1: First Steps in the World of Online Trading 10

    What is Online Trading? 10

    The History of Online Trading 13

    Advantages of Online Trading 15

    Risks of Online Trading 16

Chapter 2: Basic Concepts 18

    Financial Markets: Description and Functionality 20

    Financial Instruments: Stocks, Bonds, Cryptocurrencies, Futures, and Options 27

Chapter 3: Starting with Online Trading 42

    What is a Trading Platform? 44

    What is the Purpose of a Trading Platform? A Comprehensive Look 46

    Opening a Trading Account: Steps and Requirements 50

Chapter 4: Understanding the Stock Market and Forex 60

    Differences Between the Stock Market and Forex 61

Chapter 5: Japanese Candlesticks: A Guide to Successful Patterns 72

Chapter 6: Market Analysis 97

    Technical Analysis 98

    Fundamental Analysis: A Deep Dive into Financial Evaluation 108

Chapter 7: Trading Strategies 117

Beginner Strategies: Trend Trading, Breakout Trading, and News Trading 118

Strategies for Intermediates: Swing Trading, Scalping and Day Trading 129

Chapter 8: Risk Management 144

How to Calculate Risk and Position Sizing 147

Market Considerations and Asset Types 152

Chapter 9: Leverage 155

How Financial Leverage Works 157

Leverage Risks in Focus 160

Chapter 10: The Psychology of Trading 167

Chapter 11: Developing a Trading Plan 172

Chapter 12: Technological Innovation in Trading 178

Chapter 13: Fundamental Trading Terminologies 185

Conclusion 188

Introduction

The art of trading, with its infinite nuances and promises of financial freedom, has always captivated those who seek not only to grow their wealth but also to uncover the secrets governing the financial markets. However, this journey is filled with challenges and obstacles that demand not only knowledge and strategy but also a profound sense of discipline and remarkable psychological resilience.

Imagine navigating the turbulent markets with the confidence of someone who deeply understands the tools at their disposal, capable of interpreting the signals preceding major price movements, and positioning yourself decisively at the right moment. Trading then ceases to be a game of chance and becomes a conscious choice—an outcome of refined skills and a well-crafted strategy.

This guide has been created to provide a clear introduction to trading for beginners while offering advanced insights for those who already have experience in the field. Together, we will explore the fundamentals of trading, analyze the workings of financial markets, delve into the principles of fundamental and technical analysis, understand the importance of risk management, and uncover the impact of psychology on trading decisions.

But trading is also a story of people, of dreams, and of personal goals. Every trader embarks on a unique journey marked by achievements and lessons. Within these pages, you will find the tools to write your own chapter in this fascinating world, learning to move skillfully through charts and figures, decipher market trends, and build a strategy that reflects your personal vision of success and financial freedom.

With an approach that balances theory and practice, this book aims to guide you step by step in building a solid foundation of knowledge, enriched by practical examples, case studies, and tested strategies. It is a journey that demands commitment and dedication but promises to equip you with the skills to confidently navigate the trading market, turning uncertainty into opportunity and knowledge into power.

The journey into the world of trading begins with the first step. Are you ready to take it?

Chapter 1: First Steps in the World of Online Trading

What is Online Trading?

Online trading, in its broadest sense, is the buying and selling of financial instruments through internet platforms provided by intermediaries or online brokers. This method of interacting with financial markets has radically transformed the way individuals and investors access and operate in global markets. No longer confined to traditional trading methods that required phone calls to physical brokers or attendance on the trading floor, investors can now execute financial transactions from anywhere in the world, as long as they have an internet connection.

One of the most significant transformations brought by online trading is the democratization of access to financial markets. Before the advent of online trading, participating in the financial markets was often seen as an arena reserved for institutional investors or those with substantial capital and connections in the financial world. However, the emergence of online trading platforms has opened the doors to a much wider audience, enabling individual investors with limited capital to actively participate in trading.

Online trading platforms open the door to a vast universe of financial instruments, offering investors virtually unlimited opportunities to diversify their portfolios and seek returns. Through these platforms, users can easily access and trade stocks, which represent corporate ownership and offer a share of ownership in a company. Bonds, issued by government or corporate entities to finance their operations, provide another dimension of investment, offering returns in the form of interest.

Cryptocurrencies, digital assets that leverage cryptography to secure transactions and control the creation of new units, have added a new frontier for speculation and investment. Commodities such as gold, oil, or wheat, traded on global markets, offer additional opportunities for diversification. Finally, Forex, the foreign exchange market, represents the largest financial market in the world by trading volume, allowing investors to speculate on currency fluctuations.

Online trading has rapidly gained popularity among investors worldwide due to its numerous advantages. The convenience of accessing online trading platforms 24/7 allows traders to operate in global markets at any time, offering unprecedented flexibility. This direct control over one's trades, with the ability to execute transactions in real-time, radically changes the dynamics of investing, placing traders in command of their financial decisions. Furthermore, competition among platforms has significantly reduced transaction costs, making online trading an economically advantageous choice.

Additionally, access to advanced analytical tools, real-time market data, and educational resources greatly enhances investors' decision-making capabilities, providing the necessary information to make informed trading decisions. These developments in online trading have not only made financial markets more accessible but have also transformed the way investors approach trading.

The ability to access a wide range of financial instruments, benefit from direct control over one's trades, and enjoy reduced costs and access to informational resources has democratized trading in a way that was unimaginable just a few decades ago. This transformation has opened new possibilities for investors worldwide, emphasizing the importance of a solid financial education and prudent risk management when navigating the dynamic world of online trading.

The advent of online trading has also changed the profile of the average investor, making financial education and market awareness critical components for trading success. Investors now need to understand not only the basics of trading but also the complexities of the financial instruments they choose to trade. Furthermore, risk management and discipline have become fundamental skills, as online trading offers both significant profit opportunities and the potential for rapid losses.

Online trading has irreversibly transformed the way people invest, offering unparalleled freedom and opportunities. However, this freedom comes with the responsibility to educate oneself and operate with prudence and awareness. The key to making the most of the opportunities offered by online trading lies in the combination of a solid financial education, rigorous risk management, and a continuous quest for knowledge. In this way, investors can not only protect their capital but also thrive in a constantly evolving market environment.

The History of Online Trading

Online trading, as we know it today, began to take shape in the 1990s, a decade that marked the digital transformation of many economic and financial activities. This shift was driven by a series of technological and regulatory innovations that made it possible to execute financial transactions over the internet.

The real breakthrough occurred in the early 1990s, when the internet became accessible to the general public. In 1991, the National Science Foundation (NSF) lifted the ban on the commercial use of the internet, paving the way for the emergence of the first online businesses. It was in this context that the first online trading platforms began to appear, albeit in a much more primitive form than today's standards.

One milestone during this period was the introduction of the first electronic trading system, NASDAQ, as early as the 1970s, which laid the groundwork for future online trading. However, it was only with the advent of the internet that the concept of online trading as we know it today began to take shape.

As internet access expanded into homes in the mid-1990s, companies like E*TRADE and Charles Schwab began offering online trading services, revolutionizing the way individuals accessed financial markets. These platforms allowed users to buy and sell stocks with just a few clicks, eliminating the need to interact directly with a broker.

In 1996, E*TRADE launched one of the first entirely online advertising campaigns, drawing public attention to the potential of online trading. This period also saw the introduction of important technological advancements, such as web-based trading platforms, which provided even more direct and immediate access to financial markets.

By the turn of the millennium, online trading had established itself as a fundamental component of the global financial system. The dot-com bubble of 2000-2001 tested the industry but also contributed to strengthening regulations and improving technological infrastructures, making online trading more secure and reliable.

In subsequent years, the rise of social media and the development of mobile devices further democratized access to online trading, enabling investors to trade from anywhere at any time. This led to a diversification of financial instruments available for online trading, from traditional stocks and bonds to cryptocurrencies and contracts for difference (CFDs).

Today, online trading is an indispensable component of the financial world, with millions of retail investors accessing global markets via smartphones, tablets, and computers. Transparency, reduced transaction costs, and real-time access to market information continue to be the pillars that underpin the appeal of online trading for modern investors.

The history of online trading is a testament to the transformative impact of technology on financial markets. From an activity exclusive to a privileged few, trading has become accessible to a global audience, offering unprecedented opportunities for financial investment and speculation.

Advantages of Online Trading

Online trading has revolutionized the way we access financial markets, offering a range of benefits that have radically transformed investment opportunities for people around the world. One of the most significant aspects of this revolution is the unprecedented accessibility to markets. With just an internet connection, individuals from every corner of the globe can now explore and invest in a wide variety of financial instruments.

This democratization of investment has opened doors that were once reserved for a select group of well-connected or institutional investors. Simultaneously, competition among online trading platforms has driven a significant reduction in fees and general trading expenses. This trend toward lower costs makes trading much more accessible and affordable for the average investor, contrasting with the traditional financial landscape, often burdened by high fees and complex cost structures.

Additionally, online trading grants investors a level of control and flexibility previously unimaginable. The ability to execute trades almost instantaneously allows investors to capitalize on market opportunities as they arise, empowering them to manage their portfolios with unprecedented precision and responsiveness. This immediate reactivity is complemented by access to advanced analytical tools, real-time market data, and a wealth of educational resources that support informed investment decisions, enabling a deeper understanding and analysis of financial markets.

Risks of Online Trading

However, the advantages of online trading also come with a downside. The ease and speed with which trades can be executed may sometimes encourage over-trading or hasty decisions, particularly in highly volatile market conditions. Such behaviors can significantly increase the risk of losses, especially for those who may be tempted to react impulsively to market fluctuations.

Another notable risk is related to online security. In the digital age, safeguarding financial and personal information is of paramount importance, and online trading platforms are no exception. Investors must be diligent in protecting their data, aware that online security requires active effort to avoid potential breaches.

Unlimited access to data and news can also lead to information overload, making it challenging for investors to filter out the noise and focus on what truly matters. This abundance of information can be overwhelming, resulting in indecision or, worse, poorly thought-out choices based on irrelevant or misleading data.

Finally, online trading demands strong personal discipline and rigorous risk management. Without these fundamental elements, investors may find themselves exposed to significant losses. While the accessibility of online trading is one of its greatest advantages, it also necessitates a balanced and thoughtful approach to safeguard capital and maximize potential opportunities for profit.

Online trading offers a world of opportunities, but these come with responsibilities and challenges. Understanding both the benefits and risks is crucial for successfully navigating the dynamic environment of online financial markets.

Chapter 2: Basic Concepts

In the journey toward understanding and mastering online trading, building a solid foundation of knowledge about the key concepts governing financial markets is essential. This chapter aims to unveil the complex and dynamic world of financial markets, exploring not only their structure and functionality but also the financial instruments that form their core. Understanding these elements is crucial for anyone who wants to navigate the sometimes turbulent waters of online trading with confidence.

We will begin with an overview of financial markets, examining their crucial role in the global economy and how they facilitate the exchange of financial resources among investors. These markets are the arena where trading operations take place, and understanding their mechanics is the first step for any trader aspiring to success. Following this, we will delve into the heart of online trading: financial instruments.

From stocks, which represent ownership shares in a business, to bonds, which reflect loans made to issuers; from cryptocurrencies, the new frontier of digital investment, to futures and options, derivative instruments that present unique opportunities and challenges. Each instrument has distinct characteristics, risks, and opportunities, and a thorough understanding of them is indispensable for developing effective trading strategies.

But what does it actually mean to invest and trade in this context?

We will discuss the distinction between these two often-confused concepts, emphasizing how understanding one's motivations and goals can influence the approach to the market and the choice of financial instruments. Investing focuses on gradually building wealth over the long term, while trading aims to capitalize on price fluctuations in the short term.

Both require knowledge and strategy but differ significantly in methods and mindset. Through this chapter, we aim to provide a fundamental and comprehensive understanding of the principles governing online trading, equipping readers with the tools necessary to confidently navigate the trading world. With these key concepts firmly in place, you will be better prepared to face the challenges of online trading and seize the opportunities financial markets offer every day.

Financial Markets: Description and Functionality

Financial markets are the infrastructure that enables the issuance, exchange, and settlement of financial instruments. They serve as venues (virtual or physical) where capital, in the form of money or securities, is exchanged between investors, institutions, and other market participants. Their existence is crucial for the functioning of the global economy as they facilitate the flow of capital and price formation, enabling businesses to raise funds and investors to allocate resources efficiently.

Financial markets represent the ecosystem where participants can buy, sell, trade, and speculate on various types of financial instruments. These markets are fundamental to the global economy as they facilitate the flow of capital and the redistribution of risk among economic actors. Understanding the different types of financial markets is essential for anyone venturing into the world of trading and investment, as each market has its specificities, rules, and dynamics. Let's explore these categories in more detail:

Stock Markets (Capital Markets)

Stock markets, also known as capital markets, are perhaps the most familiar to the general public. Here, company shares are freely bought and sold. These markets not only provide businesses with a vital channel to raise capital from investors in exchange for ownership stakes but also offer investors the opportunity to participate in companies' future profits. Stock exchanges like the New York Stock Exchange (NYSE) or NASDAQ are prime examples of stock markets where billions of dollars move daily.

Bond Markets

Unlike stock markets, bond markets are where bonds, a form of debt, are traded. When a government or corporate entity issues a bond, it essentially borrows capital from investors, offering periodic interest payments and the return of principal upon maturity. These markets are crucial for funding public and private operations, from building infrastructure to business expansion.

Commodity Markets

Commodity markets involve the trading of physical or primary goods like metals, energy, and agricultural products. These markets are vital to global economic stability, influencing everything from industrial production to consumer prices. Commodities trading can be conducted through futures contracts, options, or other derivative instruments, allowing investors to speculate on future price movements of these essential goods.

Forex Markets (Foreign Exchange)

The Forex market, or foreign exchange market, is the largest financial market in the world, with daily trading volumes exceeding $5 trillion. This global, decentralized market is where foreign currencies are traded, essential for international trade and investment. Investors and traders engage in Forex to speculate on exchange rate fluctuations, leveraging the relative value changes between currencies.

Derivative Markets

Finally, derivative markets offer financial instruments whose value is derived from other underlying assets, such as stocks, bonds, commodities, or currencies. These markets enable participants to hedge against price risks or speculate on future price movements of underlying assets. Futures, options, swaps, and contracts for difference (CFDs) are common examples of derivatives traded in these markets.

Each type of financial market plays a unique role in the global economy, offering different opportunities and risks for investors. A deep understanding of these markets is fundamental for successfully navigating the world of investments, allowing investors to diversify portfolios, manage risk, and seize profit opportunities in various economic and market environments.

Functioning of Financial Markets

The functioning of financial markets, while rooted in the fundamental principles of supply and demand, reveals a complexity and sophistication that goes far beyond this basic mechanism. The pricing of financial instruments, influenced by investors' collective expectations about their future value, represents only the tip of the iceberg of a vast and multifaceted system. Let's dive deeper into some of the key aspects that contribute to the dynamic operation of financial markets.

Financial intermediaries, such as banks, brokers, and investment firms, play a crucial role in the financial market system. Acting as bridges between investors and markets, these intermediaries not only facilitate transactions but also offer a wide range of services, including investment advice, risk management, and asset custody. Through their activities, intermediaries help enhance market efficiency by ensuring liquidity and facilitating the meeting of supply and demand.

Regulation plays a fundamental role in maintaining the integrity and stability of financial markets. Regulatory bodies at the national level, such as the Securities and Exchange Commission (SEC) in the United States or the Financial Conduct Authority (FCA) in the United Kingdom, along with international organizations, establish rules and standards that market participants must follow. These regulations are designed to protect investors, ensure transaction transparency, and prevent financial fraud and abuse. Through constant monitoring and the ability to impose penalties, regulators ensure that markets operate fairly and efficiently.

Technological advancements have revolutionized the financial market landscape, increasing accessibility and dramatically changing the way transactions are conducted. Digitalization has enabled the creation of online trading platforms, offering investors the ability to execute trades in real time from anywhere in the world. Similarly, the introduction of automated trading algorithms has paved the way for new investment strategies, allowing operations based on complex mathematical models and high-speed data analysis. These technologies have not only increased the speed and efficiency of trading but also made markets more competitive and innovative.

Innovation in financial markets extends beyond technology to include the development of new financial instruments. Derivatives, synthetic securities, and structured products are just some examples of how financial ingenuity has created investment opportunities and risk management tools previously unimaginable. These new instruments require a deep understanding and careful management, as they can involve higher levels of risk and complexity compared to traditional instruments.

The functioning of financial markets results from the interaction of a wide range of factors, from financial intermediaries facilitating trades to regulation ensuring transparency and investor protection, to technological innovation that continually transforms the way we operate in markets. This complexity underscores the importance of investors enhancing their knowledge and understanding of financial markets—not only to navigate successfully in this environment but also to take advantage of the many opportunities it offers.

Importance of Financial Markets

The importance of financial markets in the architecture of the modern economy is invaluable, serving as pillars for numerous critical functions that sustain not only economic growth but also the stability and efficiency of the global financial system. These markets are far more than mere venues for trading; they are sophisticated mechanisms facilitating a range of processes vital to the economic well-being of nations and individual investors. Let's take a closer look at their key roles and societal impact.

Financial markets are essential for directing savings toward the most productive investments. Without these markets, capital might end up in low-return enterprises or projects, hindering economic growth and innovation. Through a natural selection process, where only the most compelling and profitable proposals attract investment, financial markets ensure that capital is used in the most efficient way possible, driving economic development and promoting technological and industrial advancement.

The price determination function of financial markets is crucial for the efficient allocation of resources. These markets provide a constant flow of real-time prices that reflect investors' collective valuations of assets, based on current information, future forecasts, and risk assessments. This pricing mechanism helps investors make informed decisions, allowing them to evaluate the current value of investments and anticipate future market movements.

Financial markets offer investors advanced tools for risk management, such as derivatives, which allow hedging against price fluctuations and other types of financial risks. This functionality is vital for businesses seeking to protect their balance sheets from adverse changes in interest rates, exchange rates, or commodity prices. The ability to diversify investments across a wide range of assets and markets is another critical aspect of risk management, enabling investors to reduce portfolio volatility and improve risk-adjusted returns.

The liquidity provided by financial markets—the ability to quickly convert investments into cash without significant loss of value—is essential for financial flexibility. This aspect is particularly important during times of uncertainty or financial need, as it ensures that investors can easily access their funds. Liquidity also contributes to the stability of the financial system, preventing liquidity crises that could lead to bank failures or broader economic downturns.

Financial markets play an irreplaceable role in supporting and promoting the health of the global economy. They facilitate access to capital, support risk management, contribute to economic stability, and promote the efficient allocation of resources. Acting as catalysts for growth, innovation, and shared prosperity, they empower businesses, governments, and individuals to achieve their full potential. By channeling resources efficiently and fostering resilience, financial markets drive advancements that shape a more sustainable and equitable global economy.

Financial Instruments: Stocks, Bonds, Cryptocurrencies, Futures, and Options

The world of financial markets is populated by a variety of financial instruments, each with unique characteristics, risks, and opportunities. These instruments form the beating heart of the financial system, enabling businesses to raise funds, investors to allocate capital, and market participants to manage risk. Let's explore the main categories of financial instruments in greater detail: stocks, bonds, cryptocurrencies, futures, and options.

Stocks: Ownership and Growth Potential

Stocks represent shares of ownership in a company made available to the public through stock markets. Purchasing stocks means becoming a co-owner of a business, even if only to a small extent. This ownership offers the potential to benefit economically from the company's growth and success while often conferring voting rights that allow shareholders to influence corporate decisions during annual meetings.

Shareholders, as partial owners of a company, are typically entitled to receive a portion of the profits distributed as dividends. The frequency and amount of these dividends vary depending on the company's financial health and distribution policies. Additionally, in the event of the company's liquidation, shareholders have a right to claim a portion of any remaining assets, though only after all other financial obligations have been met.

Investing in stocks is often considered a powerful avenue for achieving higher returns compared to other financial instruments, such as bonds. The growth and success of a company can lead to a significant appreciation in stock value. For instance, early investors in tech giants like Apple or Amazon witnessed exponential growth in the value of their shares, reflecting these companies' extraordinary success and global expansion.

However, stock investments also come with substantial risks. Stock markets are notoriously volatile, and stock prices can fluctuate significantly due to various factors, including company performance, general economic conditions, interest rates, geopolitical tensions, and market trends. Furthermore, in the case of bankruptcy, shareholders are the last in line for repayment, which means there is a risk of losing the entire investment.

Strategies for Navigating the Stock Market

To navigate the stock market successfully, investors must conduct thorough evaluations of the companies they wish to invest in. This includes analyzing financial statements, assessing growth prospects, understanding competitive positioning, and evaluating the company's ability to generate consistent profits.

Investors often rely on two primary methods of analysis:

1. **Fundamental Analysis**: Examining the company's financial health, including revenue, profit margins, and market position, to determine its intrinsic value.

2. **Technical Analysis**: Analyzing historical price charts and market trends to predict future movements in stock prices.

A well-informed investor looks for undervalued stocks or those with high growth potential, aligning their choices with their financial goals and risk tolerance.

Balancing Opportunities and Risks

Investing in stocks offers the opportunity to participate directly in the economic success of companies, with the potential for substantial financial rewards. However, it also demands a careful assessment of risks and the development of a well-thought-out investment strategy.

Understanding market dynamics and company fundamentals is crucial to maximizing opportunities while mitigating risks. Successful stock market participation requires discipline, knowledge, and a long-term perspective to navigate the inherent volatility and capitalize on growth opportunities.

Bonds: Stability and Predictable Returns

Bonds, which represent loans made by investors to governments or corporations, are a cornerstone of global financial markets. These debt instruments provide issuers with a means to finance new projects, manage existing debt, or support daily operations, while offering investors periodic returns in the form of interest payments, commonly known as coupons.

One of the defining features of bonds is their structure of regular interest payments until maturity, at which point the issuer repays the initial capital investment. This predictable income stream makes bonds particularly appealing to those seeking a stable and relatively safe source of income.

Key Characteristics of Bonds

- **Credit Quality**: Bonds vary in risk based on the issuer's creditworthiness, which is assessed by rating agencies such as Moody's or Standard & Poor's. High-quality bonds, such as government-issued securities from stable economies, are considered low-risk. In contrast, high-yield bonds—often referred to as "junk bonds"—offer higher returns but carry a greater risk of default.

- **Interest Rate Sensitivity**: One of the primary factors influencing bond prices is interest rate movements. When interest rates rise, the market value of existing bonds tends to decrease, as newly issued bonds offer higher yields. Conversely, falling interest rates increase the value of existing bonds with higher fixed rates, underscoring the inverse relationship between bond prices and interest rates.

- **Default Risk**: This refers to the possibility that the issuer may fail to make interest payments or repay the principal at maturity. This risk is more pronounced in bonds issued by financially weaker entities, even though they may offer higher yields.

Practical Examples

Consider U.S. Treasury Bonds, often regarded as one of the safest investments available. Backed by the full faith and credit of the U.S. government, these bonds are highly attractive to investors seeking security and stability. However, even these bonds are subject to price fluctuations due to changes in interest rates, proving that no investment is entirely without risk.

In contrast, corporate bonds from emerging companies or less stable organizations might offer enticingly high yields but come with significant default risks. Investors in these bonds must weigh the potential returns against the possibility of losing their capital.

Strategic Use of Bonds

Bonds serve multiple purposes within an investment portfolio:

1. **Income Generation**: The steady flow of interest payments makes bonds ideal for investors seeking predictable cash flow, such as retirees.

2. **Risk Diversification**: Including bonds in a portfolio can reduce overall volatility by balancing the higher-risk, higher-reward nature of equities.

3. **Capital Preservation**: High-quality bonds, especially government securities, provide a secure way to protect principal investment.

Balancing Risk and Return

Bonds are fundamental financial instruments that offer significant benefits in terms of reducing risk and generating stable income. However, a clear understanding of the factors influencing their value—such as interest rates and credit risk—is essential to maximize returns and safeguard invested capital.

For instance, in a rising interest rate environment, investors might prefer short-term bonds to mitigate price fluctuations. Conversely, in a declining rate scenario, long-term bonds with higher fixed coupons become more attractive.

Bonds, with their stability and versatility, remain a critical tool for achieving financial goals, whether it be steady income, capital preservation, or portfolio diversification. However, careful selection and monitoring of bond investments are crucial for navigating the complexities of the bond market and maximizing potential benefits.

Cryptocurrencies: The Digital Frontier of Finance

Cryptocurrencies represent one of the most significant and disruptive innovations in modern finance. Born from the idea of creating a completely digital and decentralized form of money, these currencies leverage advanced technologies such as blockchain to ensure security, transparency, and independence from central authorities like banks and governments. The cryptography at the core of cryptocurrencies serves two primary purposes: securing transactions and controlling the creation of new units of currency, a process known as "mining."

This approach to digital security has earned cryptocurrencies the trust of many investors, even in the absence of a central regulatory authority.

Key Cryptocurrencies and Their Unique Features

- **Bitcoin**: Introduced in 2009, Bitcoin pioneered this new frontier and remains the most well-known and valuable cryptocurrency. It operates as a decentralized digital currency, allowing peer-to-peer transactions without intermediaries.

- **Ethereum**: Following Bitcoin, Ethereum introduced not only a digital currency (Ether) but also a platform for executing "smart contracts" and building decentralized applications. This innovation expanded the utility of cryptocurrencies beyond simple transactions.

- **Ripple (XRP)**: Focused on revolutionizing international financial transactions, Ripple aims to provide faster and cheaper cross-border payment solutions compared to traditional systems.

The Volatility of Cryptocurrencies

Volatility is a hallmark of cryptocurrencies, with prices subject to dramatic and sudden fluctuations. Factors such as public adoption, government regulations, technological advancements, and market sentiment drive this instability. While volatility creates opportunities for significant profits, it also introduces substantial risks, making cryptocurrencies more suitable for those with a high risk tolerance and a well-thought-out investment strategy.

Example

Bitcoin's price history exemplifies the dramatic swings in value typical of cryptocurrencies. Early adopters who purchased Bitcoin shortly after its launch experienced exponential growth in their holdings over time. However, this journey has been marked by sharp declines and periods of intense market correction, testing the resilience of investors.

The Evolving Landscape of Cryptocurrencies

The cryptocurrency market is continually evolving, with new projects and tokens regularly emerging, each bringing its own set of promises and challenges. Some cryptocurrencies aim to revolutionize specific sectors or applications, while others seek to enhance or expand on concepts introduced by Bitcoin and Ethereum.

- **Smart Contracts**: Ethereum's blockchain facilitates programmable contracts that execute automatically when predefined conditions are met.

- **Decentralized Finance (DeFi)**: A growing sector within cryptocurrency that aims to recreate traditional financial services—such as lending, borrowing, and trading—on blockchain platforms without intermediaries.

Regulation remains a major area of uncertainty and potential disruption. Governments worldwide are still exploring the best ways to address this new asset class, balancing the need for investor protection with fostering innovation.

Strategic Considerations for Cryptocurrency Investments

Investing in cryptocurrencies requires a cautious approach:

1. **Understanding the Technology**: Investors should familiarize themselves with blockchain, mining, and the mechanisms underlying each cryptocurrency.

2. **Diversification**: Spreading investments across multiple cryptocurrencies can help mitigate the risks associated with any single asset.

3. **Risk Management**: Setting clear investment limits and preparing for high volatility are essential strategies for safeguarding capital.

The Future of Cryptocurrencies

Cryptocurrencies represent an exciting financial frontier offering unique opportunities for investment and innovation. However, their high volatility and associated risks demand careful planning, a deep understanding of underlying mechanisms, and a strategic approach to investing.

As the cryptocurrency sector continues to evolve, it promises to challenge traditional financial conventions and open pathways to new economic and technological growth. Whether as a speculative asset or a tool for decentralization, cryptocurrencies are reshaping the financial landscape in unprecedented ways.

Futures: Navigating Price Fluctuations with Strategy

Futures contracts are among the most dynamic and versatile categories of financial derivatives. Their primary function is to help investors and businesses manage exposure to future price risks of underlying assets. Through a legal agreement, parties commit to buying or selling a specified asset at a predetermined price on a future date. This mechanism provides an effective way to anticipate and neutralize undesirable market fluctuations.

Key Functions of Futures

1. **Hedging**
   Hedging is a strategy primarily used by producers, farmers, and businesses to shield themselves from

price fluctuations that could negatively impact their financial performance. For example, a farmer may sell futures contracts on wheat to lock in a fixed price for their future production, thereby mitigating the risk of a price drop during harvest season.

2. **Speculation**

    Speculators use futures contracts to profit from price movements of underlying assets. Since futures require only a fraction of the contract's value as an initial margin, they offer opportunities for substantial gains—or losses—with relatively limited capital. This leverage makes futures attractive but inherently risky.

Underlying Assets

Futures contracts can be based on a diverse range of assets, including:

- **Commodities**: Such as oil, gold, wheat, and coffee. These contracts are essential for businesses that require predictability in the costs of raw materials.

- **Stock Indices**: Allowing traders to speculate on the future directions of global equity markets or hedge against potential downturns.

- **Interest Rates**: Used to manage exposure to fluctuations in interest rates, which can affect the value of various financial products.

Risks Associated with Futures

While futures offer significant opportunities for both hedging and speculation, they carry substantial risks:

- **Market Risk**: If prices move in the opposite direction of an investor's expectations, losses can exceed the initial investment.
- **Leverage Risk**: The use of leverage can amplify both gains and losses, making futures high-risk instruments.
- **Volatility**: Futures markets can be highly volatile, requiring constant monitoring and quick decision-making.

Practical Example

Consider a coffee producer anticipating a decline in prices over the next few months. By selling coffee futures, the producer locks in a guaranteed sale price, protecting themselves from a potential drop in value. Conversely, a speculator expecting prices to rise may buy coffee futures, aiming to sell the contracts later at a higher price for profit.

Strategic Use of Futures

Futures are powerful yet complex instruments that demand a deep understanding of their mechanics and the underlying markets. When used correctly, they can provide effective strategies for hedging and speculation. However, investors must be acutely aware of risks, particularly those related to leverage and market volatility.

Futures are not suitable for all investors, but for those equipped with the necessary knowledge and discipline, they offer robust tools for navigating the uncertainties of financial markets.

Options

Options are financial derivatives that grant the **right**, but not the **obligation**, to buy or sell an underlying asset (such as stocks, indices, or commodities) at a pre-set price (strike price) before a specific expiration date. They are widely used for risk management, speculation, and income generation.

The Basics

- **Call Option**: The right to **buy** the asset at the strike price.

- **Put Option**: The right to **sell** the asset at the strike price.

- **Premium**: The cost paid by the buyer to the seller to acquire the option.

Options come with two key elements:

- **Strike Price**: The pre-defined price at which the asset can be bought or sold.

- **Expiration Date**: The deadline by which the option must be exercised.

For example, purchasing a call option on a stock with a strike price of $50 for a $2 premium gives you the right to buy the stock at $50. If the stock's price rises to $60, your profit is $8 ($10 gain minus the $2 premium). If the stock's price stays below $50, the option expires worthless, and you lose only the $2 premium.

Benefits:

- **Leverage**: Control larger positions with a smaller investment.
- **Flexibility**: Profit in both rising and falling markets.
- **Risk Management**: Hedge against adverse market movements.

Risks:

- **Premium Loss**: Buyers may lose the entire premium if the market moves unfavorably.
- **Unlimited Losses for Sellers**: Option sellers face potentially unlimited risk if the market moves against their position.

Practical Applications

- **Hedging**: Protect investments. For instance, buying a put option on a stock shields you from losses if its value declines.

- **Speculation**: Capitalize on price movements. A trader might buy a call option to profit from an expected price increase.

- **Income Generation**: Sell covered call options to earn premiums on stocks you already own.

Example

Suppose you own 100 shares of a stock priced at $50 each, but you're concerned the price may drop. You purchase a put option with a strike price of $48 for a $2 premium per share. If the price drops to $40, you can sell the shares at $48, protecting yourself from a larger loss. If the price remains above $48, your maximum loss is limited to the $2 premium.

Chapter 3: Starting with Online Trading

This chapter marks a pivotal moment in your exploration of online trading—a transition from theoretical learning to practical action in the vibrant world of digital financial exchanges. Here, preparation meets opportunity, guiding you from being a passionate observer to becoming an active and informed market participant. This shift represents not only a step forward in your journey of personal and financial growth but also the beginning of a phase where the decisions you make can significantly shape your trading experience.

Starting with online trading requires more than just a basic understanding of concepts; it demands a series of strategic decisions that will establish the foundation of your trading career. The first and perhaps most critical of these decisions is choosing the right trading platform. With the vast array of platforms available, each offering unique features, tools, and fee structures, selecting the ideal one becomes as much an art as a science.

We will delve into the essential criteria for making this choice, covering aspects such as usability, customer support, fees, and advanced features. These insights will help you find a platform that not only meets your current needs but also supports your long-term growth as a trader.

Opening a trading account is the next step in this journey, a process that, while appearing straightforward on the surface, often involves regulatory complexities and financial decisions. This chapter will guide you through the steps and requirements necessary to set up an account, addressing documentation, security verifications, and tax considerations to ensure a smooth transition into trading activities.

Lastly, but equally important, we will focus on the foundational concepts that form the language of online trading: market orders, limit orders, stop-loss mechanisms, and other tools that enable traders to execute strategies, manage risks, and optimize returns. These concepts are the trader's essential tools, and mastering them is critical to navigating markets successfully.

This chapter is not merely a practical introduction to online trading; it is an invitation to embark on a personal journey of discovery in the financial world. By making informed platform choices, preparing your trading account with care, and mastering the essential tools of the trade, you are moving closer to realizing your potential as a trader. You are on the brink of transforming knowledge into action, strategies into tangible results, and starting to write your own success story in online trading.

With the right approach, patience, and determination, online trading can become not just a pathway to financial goals but also a source of personal growth and deeper understanding of the forces driving the global economy. Let us prepare to explore the details of how to begin this journey, equipped with the knowledge and skills needed to approach the market with confidence.

What is a Trading Platform?

In the world of online trading, the trading platform is the centerpiece of every trader's investment ecosystem. It is not merely a tool for executing transactions; rather, it serves as an extension of the trader's analytical and operational capabilities. Understanding what a trading platform is and how it functions is the essential first step for anyone looking to navigate financial markets successfully.

At its core, a trading platform is an advanced software application that connects investors to the vast world of financial markets. It acts as a sophisticated interface, translating user strategies and commands into actionable market orders, enabling the trading of a wide range of financial instruments. These may include:

- **Stocks**: Facilitating the purchase of ownership shares in publicly traded companies.

- **Bonds**: Allowing investment in debt securities issued by governmental or corporate entities.

- **Cryptocurrencies**: Providing access to the dynamic digital currency markets.

- **Futures and Options**: Granting entry to derivative instruments for hedging or speculative strategies.

In addition to serving as a gateway for order execution, trading platforms enrich the investor experience by delivering real-time market data, an indispensable resource for informed decision-making. Users can access live quotes, interactive charts, financial news, and market analyses—all seamlessly integrated into a single environment.

Modern trading platforms are built around advanced analytical tools, which form another cornerstone of their functionality. By leveraging technical indicators, chart patterns, and fundamental analysis tools, investors can assess market potential, identify investment opportunities, and craft trading strategies rooted in sound analytical foundations.

A hallmark of trading platforms is their capacity for customization. Users can tailor the interface to suit their preferences, deciding which data to display, which indicators to apply to charts, and how to organize their workspace. This adaptability ensures that the platform aligns with the unique needs and trading style of each investor.

Trading automation represents a significant evolution in platform capabilities, allowing investors to set specific parameters for the automatic execution of orders. This not only enhances operational efficiency by eliminating the need for constant market monitoring but also enables the precise implementation of complex trading strategies with discipline and consistency.

A trading platform, therefore, is much more than a tool for accessing financial markets; it is a comprehensive environment designed to empower traders at every step of their journey. With features that blend accessibility, real-time insights, advanced analytics, and automation, it provides the foundation for informed, efficient, and strategic trading in an ever-changing financial landscape.

What is the Purpose of a Trading Platform? A Comprehensive Look

Online trading platforms are the cornerstone of the modern investor's experience. They are not merely technological tools but comprehensive ecosystems designed to facilitate every aspect of the trading process. Let's delve deeper into the critical roles these platforms play.

Trading platforms break down geographical and temporal barriers, offering investors the unique opportunity to access financial markets across the globe—from Wall Street to

Tokyo, London, and beyond. Whether dealing in stocks, bonds, commodities, currencies, or cryptocurrencies, these platforms provide an incredibly wide array of investment opportunities. The ability to interact with diverse markets through a single interface not only simplifies the investment process but also paves the way for international diversification and hedging strategies.

Order Execution: Efficiency and Precision

In the digital age, speed and accuracy in order execution are paramount. Trading platforms transform investment decisions into concrete actions within fractions of a second, ensuring that orders are executed at the most favorable prices available. This speed is particularly critical in volatile markets, where conditions can shift rapidly. Moreover, features like conditional orders—stop loss and take profit—allow automated risk management, safeguarding capital against adverse market movements.

Market Analysis: The Investor's Compass

A trading platform is more than just a gateway to markets; it is also a source of knowledge and analysis. By providing advanced charting tools, technical indicators, fundamental analysis resources, and real-time financial news feeds, platforms enable investors to explore market trends, uncover opportunities, and identify warning signals. These analytical tools are indispensable for building informed and data-driven trading strategies.

Portfolio Management: Control and a Holistic View

Modern trading platforms offer sophisticated dashboards that enable users to monitor and manage their portfolios in real time, providing a comprehensive overview of performance, risk exposure, and investment composition. This holistic view is vital for making strategic decisions, such as rebalancing a portfolio or adjusting investment strategies in response to market changes or personal objectives.

Education and Resources: Building a Strong Foundation

Many trading platforms actively contribute to the financial education of their users. Through tutorials, webinars, in-depth articles, and market analyses, these educational resources are designed to enhance the knowledge of investors—from understanding basic concepts to mastering advanced trading strategies. Access to such information significantly boosts trading competence, empowering investors to navigate markets with greater confidence and awareness.

Choosing the Right Trading Platform: A Strategic Decision

Selecting a trading platform is a critical decision that goes beyond personal preference; it directly impacts operational strategies, market analysis capabilities, and the ability to dynamically manage investments. This tool becomes a trusted ally in the trading journey, essential for executing strategies, analyzing trends, and ultimately determining the success or failure of financial operations.

A key consideration is the breadth of market access the platform provides. Some platforms specialize in specific segments, such as cryptocurrencies or commodities, while others offer more universal access to global markets, including stocks, bonds, indices, and beyond. The choice depends on specific investment goals and the desired level of portfolio diversification.

The availability of advanced technical analysis tools and in-depth market research access is fundamental to making informed decisions. Platforms equipped with customizable charting tools, fundamental analysis options, and comprehensive market reports significantly enhance the ability to anticipate trends and react promptly. Additionally, platforms that offer a variety of educational resources, from webinars to training courses, allow users to continually enrich their trading skills.

The platform's user interface should not only be aesthetically pleasing but also functional and intuitive. A complicated or unresponsive interface can hinder swift order execution, especially in volatile market conditions where every second counts. The ability to customize the interface, easily access charts, reports, and analytical tools greatly enhances the trading experience.

In today's digital era, the ability to trade on the go has become indispensable. Ensure that the platform provides robust and secure mobile apps, allowing you to monitor your portfolio, execute trades, and access real-time market data wherever you are. Compatibility with various devices and operating systems ensures you stay connected to your trading activity at all times.

Regulation is a key indicator of a platform's credibility and reliability. Verify that the platform operates in compliance with the financial regulations of your country or region and is overseen by reputable regulatory bodies. The security of your funds and personal data is equally critical; investigate the platform's security measures, including data encryption, protection against cyber-attacks, and customer safeguarding policies.

Choosing a trading platform is not merely a preliminary step into online trading; it is a decision that will profoundly influence your investment approach, your ability to adapt to evolving markets, and your overall experience as a trader. Take the time to carefully evaluate your options, considering every aspect—from functionality and costs to security and customer support.

Opening a Trading Account: Steps and Requirements

Entering the world of online trading begins with a critical step: opening a trading account with an online broker. This decision marks the official start of your trading journey and lays the foundation for your future investment experiences. Selecting a reliable and regulated broker is essential to ensure a secure and compliant platform for your financial operations.

The process starts with choosing the right broker, a decision that requires careful consideration beyond merely comparing fees. Regulation, platform usability, cost structures, customer support, and educational tools are all critical factors. A regulated broker ensures transparency and security, while a platform with intuitive design and robust features enhances the trading experience. Additionally, the availability of responsive customer support and comprehensive educational resources reflects a broker's commitment to client success.

Once the broker is chosen, the next step involves filling out an online application form, providing personal information such as name, address, and email, along with financial details and trading experience. Honesty and accuracy are crucial during this phase, as the information is used to set up the account and complete security checks.

The account opening process also includes identity verification, known as KYC (Know Your Customer), a mandatory step to prevent money laundering and financial fraud. You'll need to submit official documents, such as a government-issued ID and proof of residence, ensuring compliance and safeguarding your account.

After verification, an initial deposit is required to activate the account. Brokers typically offer multiple funding options, including credit cards, bank transfers, and e-wallets.

Consider processing times and potential fees when selecting your preferred method.

With a funded account, you gain access to the trading platform. Take time to familiarize yourself with its features, including analytical tools, customizable options, and order placement functionalities. Many platforms also offer demo accounts, allowing you to practice trading in a risk-free environment before committing real funds.

Finally, make use of the educational resources provided by the broker. Tutorials, webinars, e-books, and market analyses are invaluable for expanding your knowledge and refining your strategies. Continuous learning is fundamental to long-term trading success.

Opening a trading account, while seemingly complex, is a foundational step toward becoming an active trader. Carefully selecting a broker, completing the verification process, and mastering the trading platform establish a solid starting point for a secure and productive trading career. Success in trading stems not only from choosing the right investments but also from thorough preparation and ongoing education.

Basic Trading Concepts: Market Orders, Limits, Stop-Loss

Online trading provides a variety of tools for executing investment strategies with precision. Market orders, limits, and stop-loss mechanisms are essential for managing both entry and exit positions effectively. These tools are integral for traders aiming to navigate financial markets confidently.

Market Orders

A market order is a straightforward tool that enables traders to buy or sell assets at the best available price at the time of execution. It is ideal when speed is a priority over price precision. The simplicity of market orders makes them a go-to option for both novice and experienced traders, especially in volatile markets.

While market orders guarantee execution, they do not control the price, potentially leading to slippage in fast-moving markets. Traders must weigh the benefits of immediate execution against the risks of price deviation.

Limit Orders

Limit orders allow traders to specify the maximum purchase price or the minimum selling price for an asset. This provides greater control over the terms of the trade, making them suitable for strategies requiring precise entry or exit levels. However, there's no guarantee of execution if the market does not reach the specified price, which could result in missed opportunities.

Stop-Loss Orders

Stop-loss orders are protective tools that limit potential losses on open positions. By setting a specific price level, traders can ensure their investments are sold automatically if the market moves against them. This mechanism reduces emotional decision-making and offers peace of mind, particularly during periods of high market volatility.

One potential downside of stop-loss orders is the risk of premature execution due to temporary price fluctuations. Careful consideration of the stop-loss level is crucial to avoid unnecessary exits from potentially profitable trades.

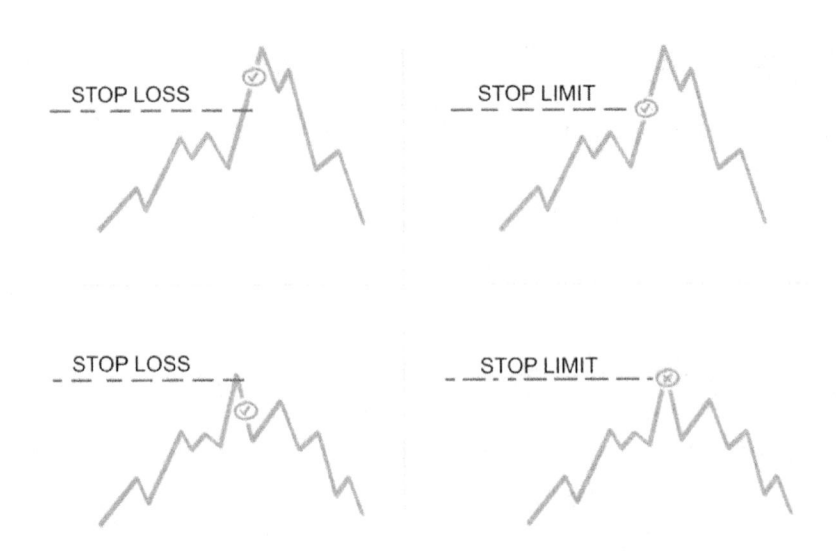

Stop-Loss Executed (top left):

In this scenario, the trader has set a stop-loss to minimize losses on a long position. When the price drops to the stop-loss level, the order is triggered, and the position is sold at the best available market price, thereby limiting further losses.

Stop-Limit Executed (top right):

Here, the trader has placed a stop-limit order. When the price reaches the stop level, a limit order is activated. The sell order is executed only if the price remains above the set limit, ensuring that the trader does not sell below this price.

Stop-Loss Not Executed (bottom left):

In this example, the price briefly reaches the stop-loss level but does not fall below it. The order is not triggered and therefore not executed, allowing the trader to stay in the position, hoping for a price recovery.

Stop-Limit Not Executed (bottom right):

Similar to the previous case, but involving a stop-limit order. Even though the price reaches the stop level, the associated limit order is not executed because the price does not reach the specified limit level for the sale, leaving the trader still in the position.

The key to successfully using these orders lies in placing them strategically, reflecting one's trading strategy and risk tolerance, while ensuring protection against market risk and the realization of profits. These examples highlight the importance of understanding market dynamics and carefully planning orders based on personal trading objectives.

```
              The Stock Rises
              Sell and Profit
                     ↖
  $9      ↑        ○   ─  ─  ─  ─
              ─ ─           ─    ─  ─
                   Take profit
  $8      ●
              ─ ─   Purchase Price
                     ─ ─
                         Stop loss
                    ○   ─  ─  ─  ─
  $7      ↓        ↙        ─  ─  ─
              The Stock Falls
              Sell and Limit Losses
```

This chart illustrates the application of 'Take Profit' and 'Stop Loss' orders in a trading context. When an investor opens a position at a price of $8, two scenarios can unfold:

1. **The Stock Rises**: If the asset's price increases, the 'Take Profit' order set at $9 allows the investor to automatically close the position and secure their gains. The 'Take Profit' order is represented by the green arrow pointing upward with a green circle, signifying the optimal exit point to maximize profits.

2. **The Stock Falls**: In the event the asset's price starts to decline, the 'Stop Loss' order set at $7 takes effect to limit losses. The red arrow pointing downward with a red circle symbolizes the 'Stop Loss' order, which is

triggered to stop further losses once the price reaches this predetermined level.

This chart emphasizes the importance of setting these orders to safeguard capital and capture profits. 'Take Profit' and 'Stop Loss' act as automated tools to close positions and are essential for a well-balanced trading strategy.

Application Strategies

The choice of order type in online trading depends on various factors, including investment goals, risk tolerance, market conditions, and trading strategy. Below are some specific scenarios where each type of order proves particularly useful:

- **Market Orders**: Ideal when execution speed takes precedence over the exact execution price. For instance, if a company announces a strategic partnership expected to significantly boost its stock value, you might want to buy immediately before prices rise further. In this case, a market order ensures you enter the position as quickly as possible.

- **Limit Orders**: Preferred when you want control over entry or exit prices, even if it means sacrificing execution immediacy. If you're monitoring a stock that you believe is overvalued and expect an imminent correction, you could set a limit sell order at the current higher price, speculating the market will reach that price before reversing its trend.

- **Stop-Loss Orders**: Essential for risk management, especially in volatile markets. If you've purchased shares of a fast-growing tech company but want protection against sudden drops, a stop-loss allows you to define the maximum loss you're willing to tolerate.

Combining Limit and Stop-Loss Orders

A strategic combination of limit and stop-loss orders can create an effective entry and exit plan that balances profit potential with risk protection. Suppose you want to buy a stock that, according to your analysis, has strong growth potential but is currently undergoing a correction:

- You can set a limit order to buy the stock at a price lower than the current one, speculating the price will drop further before recovering.

- Simultaneously, set a stop-loss order to sell the stock if the price falls below a certain level, limiting your losses should your prediction be incorrect.

Impact of Market Volatility

Market volatility is a critical factor influencing the choice and effectiveness of orders. During periods of high volatility, market orders may expose you to significant slippage, while limit orders might remain unexecuted if the price moves too quickly. Therefore, in such times, it may be wise to use limit orders to enter positions at a predetermined price and stop-loss orders to protect your capital.

Discipline is paramount in trading, and using pre-set orders can help prevent emotional decisions that might compromise your trading strategy. By setting limit and stop-loss orders in advance, according to your trading plan, you can stick to your strategy even during stressful market situations. This approach helps you stay focused on your long-term goals rather than reacting impulsively to market fluctuations.

Chapter 4: Understanding the Stock Market and Forex

This chapter marks a pivotal step toward mastering trading. Here, we leave behind the shallow waters and dive deep into the study of two financial giants: the stock market and Forex. These markets, distinct in their mechanisms but parallel in their significance, form the axis around which the trading universe revolves. While the stock market invites us to explore the realm of companies and their valuations, Forex opens the door to a global dimension where currencies move to the rhythm of national economies.

Each of these markets operates under its own set of rules, shaped by unique dynamics that influence both investment opportunities and risks. In this chapter, we will delve into the distinctive characteristics of the stock market and Forex, shedding light on how they function and what truly drives price movements. On one hand, the stock market, with its defined trading hours and sensitivity to corporate announcements and economic indicators; on the other, Forex, whose heartbeat never stops, offering trading opportunities 24 hours a day driven by global economic flows.

By understanding these fundamentals, we will be better equipped to approach volatility not as an enemy to fear but as an element to comprehend and leverage to our advantage. Get ready to discover how your trading strategy can adapt and thrive within the variety and complexity of these markets. With this chapter, we aim not only to educate but also to inspire, providing you with the knowledge needed to make informed and strategic trading decisions. Welcome to a decisive stage of your trading journey, where theory meets practice, and your skills are sharpened to successfully navigate the waves of the stock market and Forex.

Differences Between the Stock Market and Forex

The stock market represents one of the most dynamic and fundamental aspects of the global financial system, serving as a crucial meeting point for companies seeking capital and investors looking for opportunities to grow wealth and generate income. At its core, the stock market is where shares of publicly traded companies are bought and sold, making it possible for anyone to own a portion, however small, of a company.

A stock, within the context of the stock market, is more than just a financial instrument; it is a certificate of ownership that grants its holder a fraction of the issuing company. This ownership not only entitles the shareholder to a portion of the company's profits, distributed as dividends, but also provides voting rights in key corporate decisions through shareholder meetings. In this way, purchasing a company's shares becomes a direct investment in its future, with the potential to benefit from its growth and success.

Unlike globally interconnected markets such as Forex, the stock market is characterized by a strong geographical component. National exchanges, such as the New York Stock Exchange (NYSE) in the United States or the Tokyo Stock Exchange in Japan, serve as regional hubs for stock trading. Each exchange operates on its own schedule and trading hours, typically aligned with local business hours, which define the windows during which investors can trade. This structure means that regional geopolitical and economic events can have an immediate impact on local markets, influencing volatility and stock prices.

Long-Term Strategies

The stock market is often associated with long-term investment strategies. Unlike day trading or other forms of short-term speculation, investing in stocks with a long-term perspective requires a thorough evaluation of a company's financial health, growth prospects, leadership quality, and competitive position within its industry.

Short-term price movements can be influenced by speculation or emotional reactions to market news, but in the long run, a company's fundamentals drive the value of its shares. Investors adopting a long-term approach focus on identifying undervalued companies or those with growth potential not yet fully recognized by the market.

Factors Influencing Prices

Stocks, as representations of corporate ownership, reflect not only the current state of companies but also their future prospects and expectations. Understanding the factors that influence stock prices is essential for successfully navigating this dynamic environment. Quarterly and annual earnings reports offer direct insight into a company's financial health. Figures that exceed expectations can trigger an increase in stock prices, while disappointing results may lead to a significant sell-off. Investors analyze these reports not only for raw numbers but also for future forecasts and management commentary.

Revenue growth is a key indicator of a company's ability to expand its market and generate sales. An upward trajectory may indicate unrealized potential, attracting investors seeking growth opportunities. Innovations promising to revolutionize markets or new product launches can have an immediate impact on corporate valuations. Companies demonstrating consistent innovation often attract heightened attention and command higher market premiums.

Macroeconomic conditions, such as GDP growth, inflation, and unemployment rates, shape overall market sentiment and can directly impact stock prices. Periods of economic growth tend to foster optimism in equity investments, while recessions may trigger sell-offs driven by fears of future losses. Central bank decisions regarding interest rates directly influence the cost of capital. Lower rates make borrowing cheaper, potentially spurring investments and spending, which benefits companies and drives stock prices upward.

Investor sentiment can fluctuate rapidly, swayed by news, market analyses, and social trends. Public perception of a company—shaped by factors such as sustainability, social responsibility, and governance—plays an increasingly significant role in investment decisions.

The stock market is a complex and interconnected ecosystem where stock valuations result from countless variables. The ability to interpret these factors, distinguishing temporary trends from genuine growth opportunities, is what separates successful investors. Maintaining an informed approach that weighs both internal and external dynamics enables sound investment decisions based not only on current market conditions but also on the potential future of the companies being considered.

The Forex Market: An Overview

The Forex market, short for the Foreign Exchange Market, represents a vast and intricate global network where currencies from all over the world are exchanged. This market, the most liquid and largest in the world, challenges millions of traders, financial institutions, and central banks daily in a nonstop financial dance.

Unlike stock markets, which are traditionally rooted in specific geographic locations and bound by fixed trading hours, Forex boasts a ubiquitous and continuous nature. There is no central "exchange"; instead, transactions occur through an electronic network connecting participants from every corner of the globe. This characteristic ensures that, regardless of time or location, the Forex market is always in motion, offering trading opportunities around the clock.

Forex trading operates through currency pairs, expressing the value of one currency relative to another. These pairs are categorized as major, minor, and exotic, depending on their liquidity and trading volume. Every movement in Forex is essentially a bet on the relative strength of two economies, with traders analyzing and speculating on changes in currency values based on a myriad of economic, political, and social factors.

The Forex market is exceptionally sensitive to a broad range of macroeconomic and political factors. Changes in interest rates, for example, can significantly impact currency demand, as investors and speculators seek higher returns on investments denominated in certain currencies. Similarly, inflation, political stability, and overall economic performance of a nation can lead to drastic movements in currency pairs.

The inherent volatility of Forex and its 24/7 operation make it particularly suited to short-term trading strategies such as day trading or scalping. Both experienced and novice traders attempt to capitalize on minimal price fluctuations, often supported by intensive use of technical analysis and indicators to make quick and informed decisions. This dynamic nature demands constant vigilance and mental agility to effectively navigate the often turbulent waters of the currency market.

Forex offers a world of opportunities for those ready to dive into its relentless rhythm and complexities. With daily trading volumes exceeding $5 trillion, it represents a vast and vibrant financial ecosystem where deep knowledge of market mechanisms and a well-defined strategy can open the door to significant gains. However, the high leverage and volatility also pose considerable risks, making it essential to thoroughly understand both the opportunities and challenges presented by this unique market.

Factors Influencing Forex Prices

Price movements in Forex are deeply influenced by key macroeconomic indicators reflecting a nation's economic health. These include changes in GDP, employment data, trade balances, and inflation. For instance, an increase in inflation within a nation may depreciate its currency as it erodes domestic purchasing power. Similarly, employment reports showing rising job numbers can strengthen a currency, signaling robust economic growth.

Central bank decisions are among the most influential factors driving currency movements. Changes in interest rates, quantitative easing or tightening policies, and monetary policy statements can provoke significant fluctuations in exchange rates. For example, a central bank raising interest rates can attract foreign capital inflows, strengthening the national currency.

Political stability and a nation's economic performance affect risk perception and, consequently, currency movements. Countries with stable governments, predictable policies, and sound economic strategies tend to attract foreign investments, bolstering their currency. Conversely, nations experiencing political instability or economic crises often see their currency depreciate.

Investor sentiment plays a crucial role in Forex, as it does in stock markets. The overall perception of the global economy's direction or specific national economies can drive cross-border capital flows, influencing exchange rates. Additionally, geopolitical events or international crises can cause speculative movements reflecting changing perceptions.

Forex stands out as a dynamic and complex environment where understanding global macroeconomic and political factors is vital. Traders who can correctly interpret these factors and adapt their strategies accordingly can successfully navigate the Forex market, seizing opportunities presented by currency movements. The key lies in being informed, reactive, and strategic while maintaining a vigilant eye on the global economic and political horizon.

Trading Hours and Volatility

In the stock market, trading hours are closely tied to the exchanges where stocks are listed. These time windows not only indicate when trading is possible but also create periods of heightened activity and, consequently, volatility. The phenomenon known as the "opening effect," where the first and last minutes of a trading session experience elevated trading volumes, is particularly noteworthy. These moments attract both institutional and retail investors, all seeking the best opportunities before the market stabilizes or reacts to the day's news.

Stock market volatility is also amplified by the release of financial reports and significant corporate events. For example, earnings announcements can trigger sudden and substantial price movements depending on whether results meet, exceed, or fall short of market expectations. Traders and investors prepare for these events, often placing strategic orders to capitalize on or protect against anticipated price movements.

Forex: A Non-Stop Market

In contrast, the Forex market operates continuously, accessible 24 hours a day, five days a week. This unique characteristic allows traders worldwide to participate at their convenience but also introduces added complexity in terms of volatility. The overlap of trading hours between major financial hubs—such as London, New York, Tokyo, and Sydney—creates time frames of heightened volatility, offering profit opportunities for those who can correctly interpret price movements.

Moreover, Forex is highly sensitive to global economic news. Political decisions, economic reports, and international crises can cause rapid and significant fluctuations in exchange rates. Risk management thus becomes a critical component of Forex trading strategies, with the use of stop-loss and take-profit orders playing a vital role in protecting capital from unpredictable market movements.

Adapting Strategies

Given the variability of trading hours and volatility levels, traders and investors must adapt their strategies to maximize opportunities in both markets. In the stock market, it can be advantageous to focus trading activities during periods of high activity, leveraging volatility to achieve quick gains or strategically position oneself. In Forex, understanding the volatility dynamics tied to overlapping trading hours and economic news is essential for capitalizing on exchange rate fluctuations.

In conclusion, whether operating in the stock market with its defined trading hours and volatility spikes tied to corporate events, or participating in the Forex market with its continuous operation and responsiveness to global news, a deep understanding of these aspects is vital. Being informed and prepared enables traders to navigate markets with greater confidence, leveraging volatility dynamics to their advantage while adopting appropriate risk management strategies.

Case Study 1: The Stock Market and the Impact of Earnings Announcements

- **Company:** XYZ Technology

- **Event:** Quarterly earnings announcement

- **Situation:** XYZ Technology, a giant in the semiconductor industry, was expected by analysts to report a 15% revenue growth compared to the previous quarter.

- **Outcome:** Upon announcing not only a 20% revenue increase but also securing significant future contracts, the company's stock price soared by 10% within hours of the announcement.

- **Analysis:** This case highlights how earnings announcements can have an immediate impact on stock prices. Investors, anticipating strong future performance, reacted positively to the announcement, increasing demand for XYZ Technology's shares and driving up its price.

Case Study 2: Forex and the Impact of Central Bank Decisions

- **Currencies Involved:** EUR/USD

- **Event:** European Central Bank (ECB) monetary policy announcement

- **Situation:** In the context of rising inflation in the eurozone, the market was anticipating the ECB's decision on interest rates. Analysts were divided, with some predicting a rate hike to combat inflation and others expecting rates to remain unchanged to avoid stifling economic growth.

- **Outcome:** The ECB unexpectedly announced a 0.25% rate hike. The euro appreciated significantly against the US dollar, rising from 1.1200 to 1.1350 within an hour of the announcement.

- **Analysis:** This example illustrates the importance of central bank decisions in the Forex market. The rate hike made the euro more attractive to investors seeking higher returns, leading to its appreciation. The speed and magnitude of the market's reaction highlight the volatility of Forex and the importance of closely following global economic news.

These case studies offer a glimpse into the dynamics influencing the stock and currency markets, demonstrating how news and announcements can quickly alter market conditions. For traders and investors, understanding these mechanisms is crucial for developing effective strategies and successfully navigating the complexities of financial markets.

Chapter 5: Japanese Candlesticks: A Guide to Successful Patterns

Japanese candlesticks, often simply referred to as "candlesticks" in trading terminology, trace their origins back to ancient Japan. Developed in the 18th century by Munehisa Homma, a rice merchant from Osaka, they were initially used not only to record opening and closing prices but also as tools to predict market psychology. Homma discovered that, beyond the basic forces of supply and demand, traders' emotions played a crucial role in determining rice prices. Using candlesticks, he was able to chart and interpret these sentiments.

At the heart of Japanese candlestick analysis lies the understanding that each candlestick, or group of candlesticks, tells a story. These patterns represent not only the actions of buyers and sellers within a specific timeframe but also their emotions—indecision, fear, and greed. Learning to decode these stories enables traders to anticipate potential market movements with greater accuracy.

Despite their centuries-old origin, Japanese candlesticks remained relatively unknown outside Japan until the 1990s, when Steve Nison introduced them to the Western world. Since then, they have become one of the most essential tools in technical analysis, employed by traders in stocks, forex, cryptocurrencies, and other financial instruments worldwide.

Japanese candlesticks are especially valued for their ability to condense vast amounts of information into an immediately comprehensible visual format. In an era where traders must make rapid decisions based on complex data flows, the clarity of candlesticks makes them indispensable trading tools. Whether identifying potential trend reversals, confirming continuation signals, or measuring market volatility, Japanese candlesticks provide unparalleled insights into price action.

In the following sections, we will explore the structure and interpretation of Japanese candlesticks, introducing both simple and complex patterns, and discovering how they can be applied to develop sophisticated trading strategies. Through concrete examples and detailed analysis, this chapter offers a comprehensive guide to one of the cornerstones of modern technical analysis.

Japanese Candlesticks

Each Japanese candlestick represents compressed information—a visual depiction of market activity over a specified period. The structure of a candlestick is simple yet highly significant:

- **Real Body**: Represents the difference between the opening and closing prices, indicating the primary market movement during the period.

- **Shadows or Wicks**: Display the highest and lowest prices reached, revealing market volatility.

The size and color of the body, as well as the length of the shadows, provide valuable insights into market dynamics.

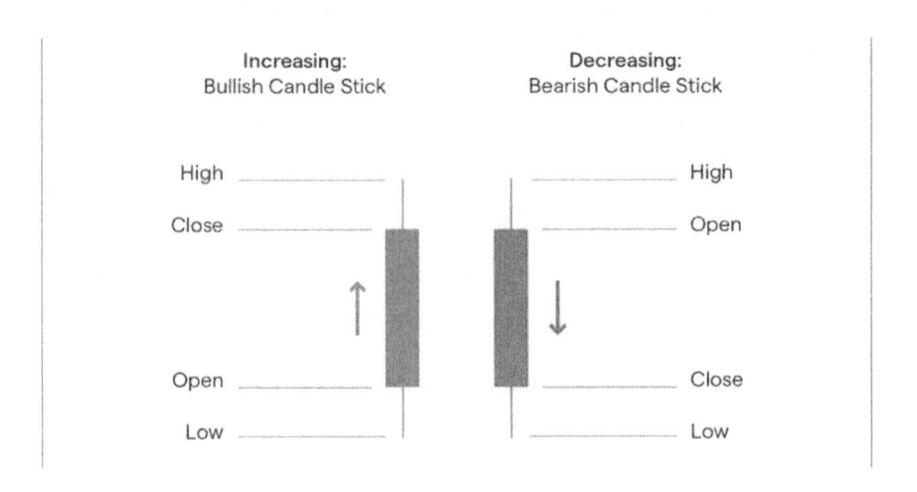

This chart provides a clear and visual representation of the basic structure of Japanese candlesticks, displaying both a bullish (green) and bearish (red) candlestick:

- **Bullish Candlestick (Green on the left)**
    - **Description**: Indicates a price increase during the represented period. The closing price is higher than the opening price.
    - **Key Elements**:
        - **Open**: The price at the start of the session.

- **Close**: The price at the end of the session.
- **High**: The highest price reached during the session.
- **Low**: The lowest price touched during the session.

- **Bearish Candlestick (Red on the right)**
  - **Description**: Indicates a price decrease. The closing price is lower than the opening price.
  - **Key Elements**:
    - **Open**: The price at the start of the session.
    - **Close**: The price at the end of the session.
    - **High**: The highest price reached.
    - **Low**: The lowest price touched.

How to Use the Chart

This chart serves as an essential tool for understanding market trends and price dynamics:

- A series of bullish candles may indicate an upward trend, signaling increased buyer activity.
- A sequence of bearish candles could point to a downward trend, with sellers dominating the market.

- The lengths of the wicks and the body provide further insights into market strength and volatility.

By using this chart as a visual reference, traders can quickly interpret market movements and incorporate these insights into their decision-making processes.

Japanese candlesticks bridge the gap between technical data and visual intuition, offering traders a powerful tool for analyzing market behavior. This chapter not only explains how to understand candlesticks but also lays the foundation for their strategic application in daily trading.

Understanding Doji Candlesticks: Patterns and Their Significance

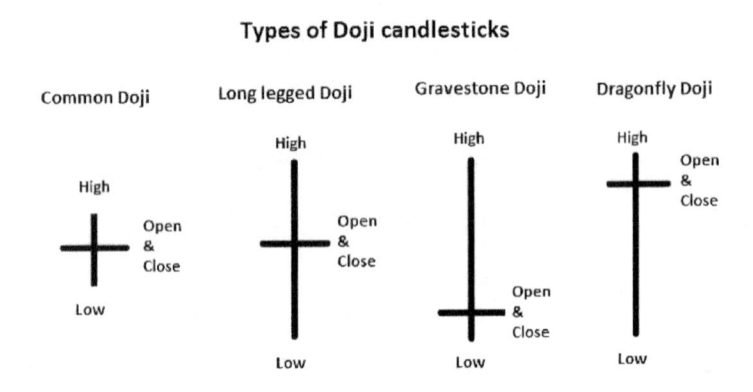

Types of Doji candlesticks

Common Doji	Long legged Doji	Gravestone Doji	Dragonfly Doji

The chart above illustrates the four main types of Doji candlesticks, each carrying unique market insights:

76

1. **Common Doji:** Represents a balance between buyers and sellers, signaling market indecision. Often found during periods of consolidation.

2. **Long-Legged Doji:** Indicates high market volatility and significant indecision. Both buyers and sellers attempted to dominate but ended in a stalemate.

3. **Gravestone Doji:** Typically a bearish reversal signal, it occurs when buyers push prices higher but fail to sustain the momentum, leading to a close near the session's low.

4. **Dragonfly Doji:** Often a bullish reversal pattern, it shows that sellers pushed prices lower but buyers regained control, resulting in a close near the session's high.

These candlestick formations are invaluable for identifying market turning points and gauging overall sentiment. By understanding their context and position within a trend, traders can make informed decisions to enhance their strategies and anticipate potential shifts in market dynamics. Recognizing the subtle differences between each Doji type allows traders to better interpret market psychology, providing deeper insights into the balance of power between buyers and sellers.

Additionally, these patterns often serve as key indicators when combined with other technical analysis tools, such as support and resistance levels, moving averages, or volume analysis. For instance, a Gravestone Doji forming near a resistance level may confirm a bearish reversal, while a Dragonfly Doji at a support zone might signal the start of an upward trend.

Incorporating Doji candlestick patterns into a broader trading plan enables market participants to navigate periods of uncertainty with greater confidence. Whether used to identify trend reversals, validate existing positions, or refine entry and exit points, these formations offer a versatile and powerful tool for traders aiming to achieve consistent results in dynamic market environments.

Hammer and Inverted Hammer Candlestick Patterns

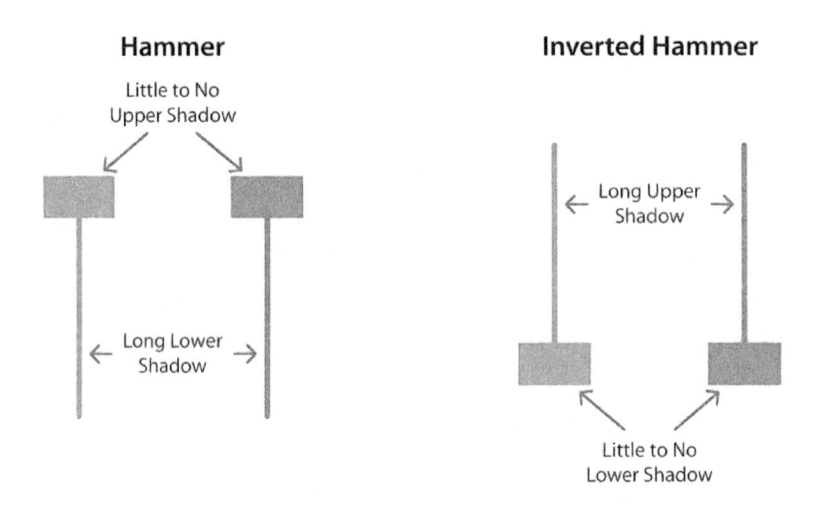

The "**Hammer**" and "**Inverted Hammer**" are two critical candlestick patterns that provide insight into potential market reversals. They are visualized in this chart, with the Hammer on the left and the Inverted Hammer on the right.

78

Hammer (Left):

- Appearance: The Hammer has a small real body near the top of the candlestick and a long lower shadow, indicating a significant low during the trading session but a strong recovery before closing.
- Interpretation: It typically signals a bullish reversal when it appears at the bottom of a downtrend. The long lower shadow reflects buying pressure overwhelming selling pressure.
- Key Features:
  o Little to no upper shadow.
  o A long lower shadow.
  o A small real body at the top.

Inverted Hammer (Right):

- Appearance: The Inverted Hammer features a small real body near the bottom of the candlestick and a long upper shadow. It appears at the bottom of a downtrend.
- Interpretation: This pattern may signal a bullish reversal, indicating hesitation among sellers and a potential shift in momentum toward buyers.
- Key Features:
  o Little to no lower shadow.
  o A long upper shadow.
  o A small real body at the bottom.

How to Use the Chart:

- When encountering these patterns:

- Look for confirmation in the subsequent candles before taking action (e.g., a higher closing price after a Hammer or Inverted Hammer suggests a reversal).
- Analyze their position within the trend: they are most effective at identifying the end of downtrends.

The Hammer on the left and the Inverted Hammer on the right are indispensable tools in any trader's analysis, especially when used alongside volume data and other technical indicators.

Bullish and Bearish Engulfing Patterns: Understanding Key Reversal Signals

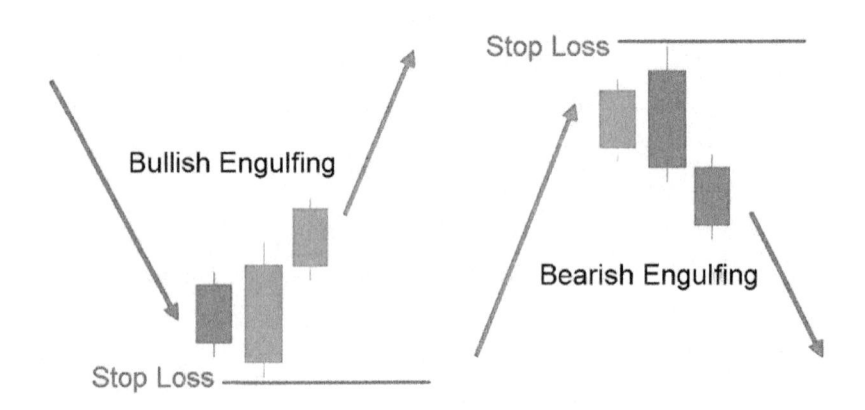

The chart illustrates two powerful reversal patterns: the *Bullish Engulfing* (left) and the *Bearish Engulfing* (right). These patterns are widely used by traders to identify turning points in market trends and capitalize on potential

80

price movements. Here's a detailed explanation of each pattern and its significance:

Bullish Engulfing Pattern (left)

The *Bullish Engulfing* appears in a downtrend and signals a potential shift toward upward momentum. This pattern is formed when a green candlestick fully "engulfs" the previous red candlestick. The size of the green candle highlights the dominance of buyers over sellers, indicating a potential reversal.

- **Key Characteristics**: The green candle opens lower than the red one but closes higher, showcasing strong buying pressure.
- **Strategic Usage**: Traders often consider entering long positions when the pattern forms and place a stop-loss below the pattern's low to mitigate risk.
- **Context**: It's most effective when supported by other indicators, such as oversold conditions or bullish divergence in momentum indicators.

Bearish Engulfing Pattern (right)

The *Bearish Engulfing* emerges in an uptrend and warns of potential downward movement. This pattern occurs when a red candlestick completely "engulfs" the prior green candlestick, reflecting increasing selling pressure.

- **Key Characteristics**: The red candle opens higher than the green one but closes significantly lower,

signaling a shift in market sentiment from bullish to bearish.
- **Strategic Usage**: Traders often take short positions following this pattern and set a stop-loss above the high of the engulfing candle to limit losses.
- **Context**: Confirmation through high trading volume or bearish divergence can strengthen the reliability of this pattern.

By mastering these patterns, traders can anticipate reversals with higher confidence and refine their strategies for both trending and range-bound markets. These candlestick formations are particularly impactful when identified at key support or resistance levels, enhancing their predictive value.

Hanging Man and Shooting Star Candlestick Patterns: Recognizing Market Reversals

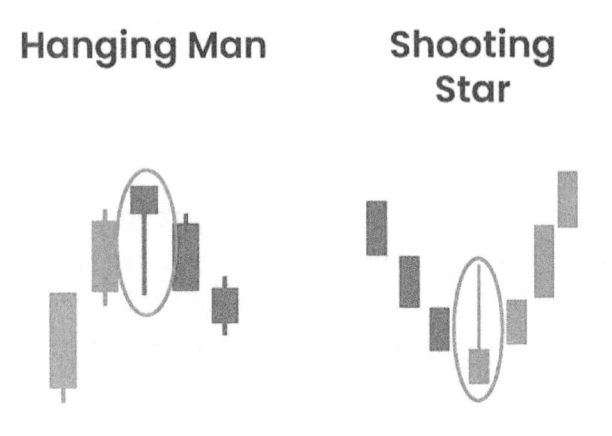

This chart highlights two prominent candlestick patterns, the *Hanging Man* (left) and the *Shooting Star* (right), both of which serve as signals of potential market reversals. These patterns are essential for traders aiming to anticipate changes in market trends.

Hanging Man (left)

The *Hanging Man* typically forms at the end of an uptrend and indicates a potential bearish reversal. It suggests that sellers are beginning to overpower buyers, even if the price closes near its high.

- **Key Characteristics**:
    - A small real body located near the top of the candlestick, which can be either red (bearish) or green (bullish).
    - A long lower shadow, at least twice the length of the real body, indicating significant selling pressure during the session.
    - Little to no upper shadow.
- **Strategic Implication**:
    - A *Hanging Man* is a warning of potential weakness in the current uptrend. Confirmation from subsequent price action, such as a lower close, is essential before taking a short position.

Shooting Star (right)

The *Shooting Star* also signals a potential reversal but appears at the end of an uptrend, marking the transition to bearish sentiment. It reflects an initial surge in buying that ultimately gets overwhelmed by sellers.

- **Key Characteristics**:
    - A small real body positioned near the bottom of the candlestick.
    - A long upper shadow, at least twice the size of the real body, showing an initial upward push followed by strong selling pressure.
    - Little to no lower shadow.
- **Strategic Implication**:
    - The *Shooting Star* warns of an impending downturn in price. As with the *Hanging Man*, traders should look for confirmation from subsequent candlesticks before entering short positions.

Usage Tips

These patterns gain reliability when observed near key resistance levels or after extended trends. Combined with volume analysis or other indicators, they provide stronger evidence of trend exhaustion and reversal.

Evening Star and Morning Star Candlestick Patterns: Indicators of Major Trend Reversals

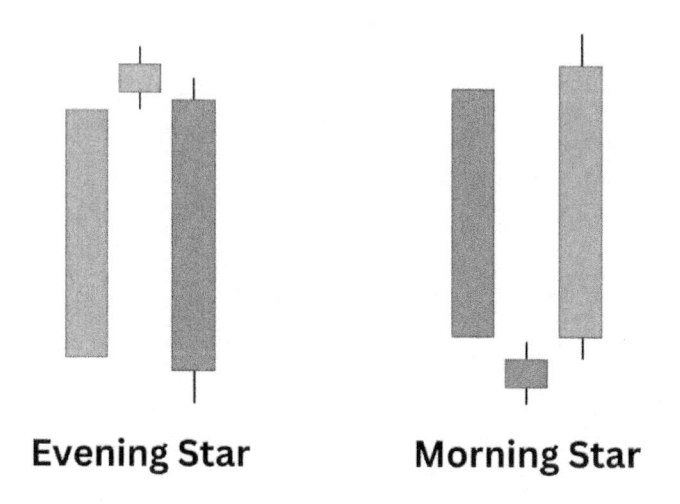

Evening Star   **Morning Star**

This chart illustrates two key candlestick patterns: the *Evening Star* (on the left) and the *Morning Star* (on the right). These patterns are highly reliable indicators of potential major trend reversals and are widely used by traders to anticipate shifts in market sentiment.

Evening Star (Left)

The *Evening Star* typically appears at the end of an uptrend, signaling a bearish reversal. It reflects a transition from bullish to bearish market sentiment.

- **Structure**:
    1. A large bullish (green) candle, indicating strong upward momentum.

2. A small-bodied candle (doji or spinning top), suggesting indecision or waning buying pressure.
   3. A large bearish (red) candle, closing well below the midpoint of the first candle, confirming the downward reversal.
- **Strategic Implication**:
   - The *Evening Star* warns traders of a potential price decline. Confirmation from further bearish candles strengthens the validity of the reversal signal.

Morning Star (Right)

The *Morning Star* is a bullish reversal pattern that forms at the end of a downtrend, indicating the start of an upward price movement.

- **Structure**:
   1. A large bearish (red) candle, reflecting strong downward momentum.
   2. A small-bodied candle (doji or spinning top), signifying market indecision or a balance between buyers and sellers.
   3. A large bullish (green) candle, closing well above the midpoint of the first candle, confirming the upward reversal.
- **Strategic Implication**:
   - The *Morning Star* suggests a potential price rise. Further bullish candles reinforce the validity of this signal.

Key Considerations

1. **Location Matters**: These patterns are most effective when observed near significant support or resistance levels.
2. **Volume Analysis**: High volume during the third candle adds credibility to the reversal signal.
3. **Trend Confirmation**: Use additional indicators or chart patterns to confirm the reliability of the signal.

Understanding Bullish Harami and Bearish Harami Patterns

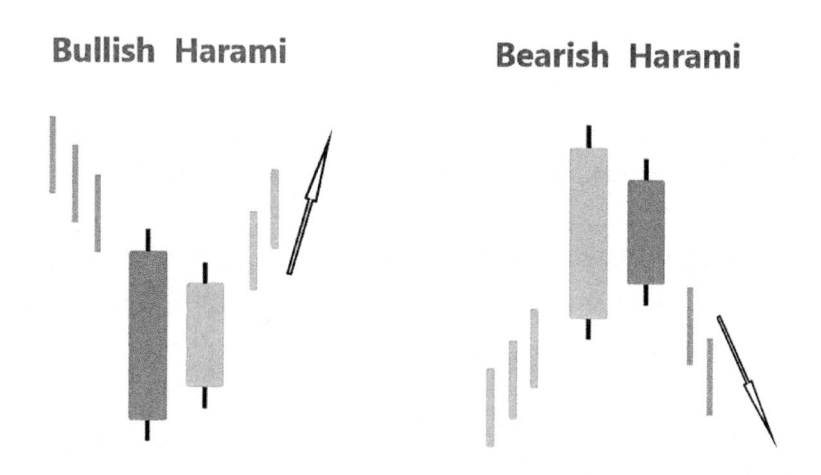

Bullish Harami

Bearish Harami

The Bullish Harami and Bearish Harami are essential candlestick patterns in technical analysis, widely used by traders to identify potential trend reversals in financial markets. Comprising two candles, these patterns offer insights into shifts in market sentiment and provide early indications of a possible change in direction.

Bullish Harami (Left Side):

- **Formation**: This pattern appears during a downtrend and signifies a possible bullish reversal. It is composed of a large red (bearish) candle followed by a smaller green (bullish) candle. The second candle is entirely contained within the body of the first, illustrating a consolidation or pause in selling momentum.
- **Indication**: The smaller green candle indicates reduced selling pressure and the emergence of buyers, suggesting a shift in control from sellers to buyers. This transition is a potential precursor to an upward trend.
- **Interpretation**: Traders often interpret this as a signal to prepare for a possible bullish movement. It may serve as an entry point for long positions, especially when confirmed by subsequent bullish price action or other indicators such as increased volume or support levels.

Bearish Harami (Right Side):

- **Formation**: This pattern emerges in an uptrend and signals a potential bearish reversal. It features a large green (bullish) candle followed by a smaller red (bearish) candle, fully enclosed within the body of the

first. This structure demonstrates a slowdown in buyer momentum.
- **Indication**: The smaller red candle reflects waning buyer strength, suggesting that sellers might regain control, possibly leading to a downward trend. This weakening of bullish momentum is often considered an early warning of a trend reversal.
- **Interpretation**: Traders view this as a cautionary signal, prompting them to evaluate short positions or lock in profits from existing long positions. When combined with confirmation from subsequent bearish candles or other technical indicators, it becomes a stronger signal for action.

Additional Notes:

- **Reliability**: Both patterns gain significance when they appear near key support or resistance levels or after prolonged trends. Their effectiveness is further enhanced when accompanied by volume spikes, indicating stronger market conviction.
- **Strategic Use**: Traders often wait for confirmation in the form of the next candle's direction before making a move. For example, a higher close after a Bullish Harami strengthens the case for a bullish reversal, while a lower close following a Bearish Harami reinforces the likelihood of a bearish turn.

These patterns are invaluable tools for traders seeking to anticipate market reversals and adjust their strategies accordingly. When analyzed within the broader context of market trends and supported by additional technical signals, the Bullish Harami and Bearish Harami can provide powerful insights for decision-making.

Three White Soldiers and Three Black Crows

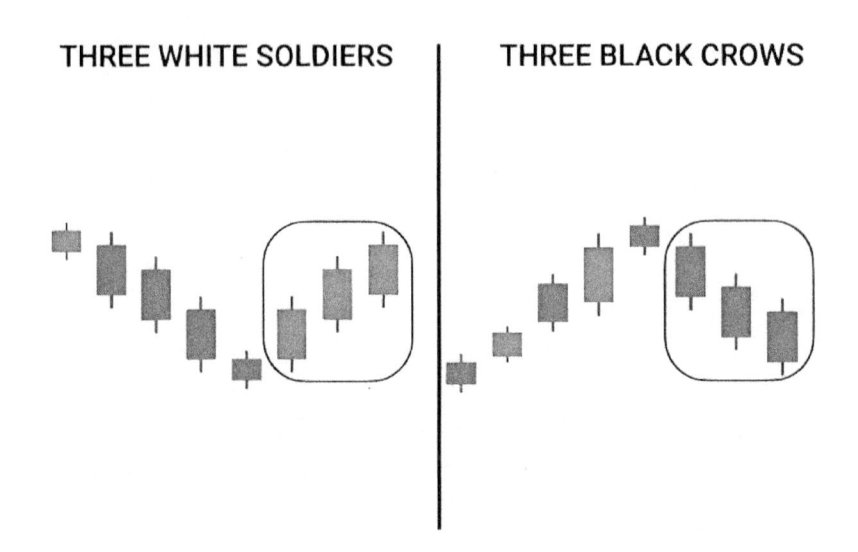

These candlestick patterns, "Three White Soldiers" and "Three Black Crows," are vital tools for traders in identifying strong trend reversals and confirming market sentiment. Here's a detailed explanation for each:

Three White Soldiers (Left Side)

- **Formation:**
  This bullish reversal pattern consists of three consecutive green candles with higher closes. Each candle opens within the previous one's body but

closes near its high, indicating steady buying pressure.

- **Indication:**
  The pattern appears after a downtrend, signaling a potential shift to a bullish trend. It reflects growing confidence among buyers.
- **Usage:**
  Traders often interpret this as a strong buy signal, especially when confirmed by increased trading volume or additional indicators like RSI.

Three Black Crows (Right Side)

- **Formation:**
  This bearish reversal pattern consists of three consecutive red candles with lower closes. Each candle opens within the previous one's body but closes near its low, signaling strong selling pressure.
- **Indication:**
  The pattern forms after an uptrend, suggesting a potential shift to a bearish trend. It indicates growing dominance by sellers and weakening buyer momentum.
- **Usage:**
  Traders use this as a sell signal or to exit long positions, particularly when it coincides with high trading volume.

Spinning Tops and Marubozu Candlestick Patterns

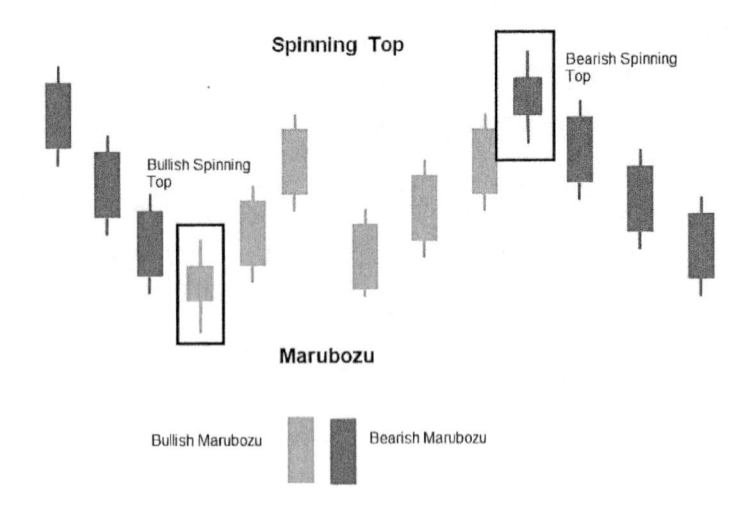

These two candlestick formations, Spinning Tops and Marubozu, are essential tools for traders looking to understand market indecision and momentum shifts. They provide a detailed glimpse into the psychology of market participants, offering clues about potential reversals, trend continuations, or periods of consolidation.

Spinning Tops

Formation:
Spinning Tops are distinguished by small real bodies that are centrally positioned between long upper and lower wicks. This structure reflects significant price movements within the session but minimal net change between the opening and closing prices.

Indication:

- **Market Indecision**: Spinning Tops signify a balance between buyers and sellers, where neither side is able to dominate.
- **Bullish Spinning Top** (Left Side): Typically appears during a downtrend and signals a potential reversal to the upside, hinting that buyer momentum may be growing.
- **Bearish Spinning Top** (Right Side): Found during an uptrend, it suggests a possible reversal to the downside, indicating weakening buyer pressure.

Usage:

Spinning Tops are not definitive reversal signals on their own but serve as warnings of potential change. Traders are advised to look for confirmation through subsequent candles or the use of complementary indicators, such as RSI (Relative Strength Index) or MACD (Moving Average Convergence Divergence).

Marubozu

Formation:

Marubozu candlesticks are unique in that they lack wicks, showcasing a full-bodied candle where the price moves unidirectionally throughout the session.

- **Bullish Marubozu (Green)**: The open price equals the low, and the close equals the high, demonstrating strong buying momentum.

- **Bearish Marubozu (Red)**: The open price equals the high, and the close equals the low, reflecting dominant selling pressure.

Indication:

- **Bullish Marubozu**: This pattern often signifies the onset of strong upward momentum, commonly appearing at the beginning of an uptrend or during a breakout.
- **Bearish Marubozu**: It indicates robust downward pressure, frequently seen at the start of a downtrend or during a breakdown of support levels.

Usage:
Marubozu candlesticks are considered powerful continuation signals. Traders use them to identify opportunities to enter trades in the direction of the prevailing trend. When accompanied by high volume or occurring near key trendlines, Marubozu patterns offer additional confirmation of their reliability.

How to Use This Chart

1. **Spinning Tops**:
    - These patterns are most effective when found near significant support or resistance levels.
    - Always wait for confirmation from the subsequent candles or combine with indicators like RSI or MACD for added confidence.
2. **Marubozu**:
    - Ideal for identifying strong trend continuation.

- Use in conjunction with existing trend analysis to confirm the direction of momentum and to time entries effectively.

By analyzing Spinning Tops and Marubozu patterns in the broader context of market conditions, traders can develop a more comprehensive understanding of price action. These candlestick formations, when used with complementary tools and strategies, empower traders to anticipate market movements with greater precision and confidence.

Concluding this chapter on Japanese candlestick patterns, it is clear how these tools, despite their centuries-old origins, remain remarkably relevant and valuable for modern traders. Japanese candlesticks are not merely graphical representations of market data but true windows into the collective psychology of buyers and sellers. Each candlestick tells a story: of battles between bulls and bears, of uncertainties, of trend confirmations or reversals, offering those who know how to interpret them a powerful ally in anticipating future price movements.

The patterns presented in this chapter, from the simple Doji to the imposing Three Black Crows, demonstrate how even the smallest variations in form and context can reveal critical information. However, like any technical analysis tool, candlesticks are not infallible. They reach their full potential when used as part of an integrated approach, combined with other technical indicators and a solid understanding of market conditions. Correctly interpreting these signals requires not only theoretical knowledge but also experience and practice—skills every trader must cultivate with patience.

It is crucial to remember that trading is not only about chart analysis but also about risk and capital management, aspects that form the backbone of a successful strategy. Japanese candlestick patterns provide valuable clues, but it is the trader, with their discipline and decision-making abilities, who turns them into concrete advantages. For those at the beginning of their journey, an important piece of advice is to practice on a demo account, exploring various patterns on historical data, to build the confidence needed before transitioning to live trading.

Chapter 6: Market Analysis

As we venture further into the core of trading, this chapter opens a new horizon of knowledge and understanding. It represents the bridge between foundational theory and advanced practical application, a crucial phase where aspiring traders learn to decode the secret language of financial markets through two of the most powerful lenses: technical analysis and fundamental analysis.

Technical analysis, with its charts, trends, support, and resistance levels, serves as a compass to navigate the storms of volatility. It provides traders with the tools to predict future market movements by analyzing historical patterns. This chapter explores the adaptability of this methodology, both in the vibrant world of Forex and the complexities of the stock market, offering a practical guide for interpreting signals that can determine the success or failure of a trading strategy.

In parallel, fundamental analysis emerges as the foundation for building a long-term investment vision. Examining corporate financial statements and economic indicators becomes an indispensable key to understanding the health and future prospects of economies and businesses. This chapter demonstrates how to skillfully apply fundamental analysis in the dynamic contexts of Forex and equity markets, emphasizing the importance of a holistic view to make well-informed investment decisions.

Finally, delving into modern analysis tools and software reveals the technological resources available to today's traders. These tools not only simplify the application of analytical techniques but also enhance the trader's capabilities, enabling the development of more sophisticated strategies and the ability to respond quickly to market changes.

Prepare to dive into a chapter that promises to be not just informative but transformative, marking a decisive step in your growth as a trader. With "Intermediate Trading Insights and Strategies," the trading world unfolds before you with new challenges and opportunities, inviting you to explore the endless paths that financial markets offer with curiosity and determination.

Technical Analysis

Technical analysis stands out as one of the cornerstones of modern trading, offering a unique and deeply analytical perspective on the direction of financial markets. This method contrasts with fundamental analysis not in terms of effectiveness but in its approach and underlying assumptions.

While fundamental analysis seeks to determine an asset's intrinsic value by examining economic data, financial reports, and other macroeconomic indicators, technical analysis assumes that all such information is already reflected in market prices. Consequently, the study of past and present price patterns is considered sufficient to predict future market dynamics.

The foundation of technical analysis lies in the belief that market prices move in identifiable trends that can be analyzed through chart observation and the use of specific mathematical tools. At the heart of this discipline is the idea that the collective behavior of market participants—driven by psychological factors, expectations, and reactions to external events—is reflected in price movements, creating predictable patterns.

Technical analysts employ a vast arsenal of tools to decode the hidden messages in price movements:

- **Charts**: Essential for visualizing historical and current price data, charts serve as the canvas on which technical analysts paint their analyses. Whether line charts, bar charts, or Japanese candlestick charts, each type offers specific visual insights into price movements, helping to identify trends, patterns, and potential reversal points.
- **Trends**: The concept of trends is fundamental to technical analysis. Recognizing whether the market is moving in an upward, downward, or sideways trend allows analysts to make predictions about future

price movements and devise trading strategies accordingly.
- **Support and Resistance Levels**: These terms describe the price levels where an asset tends to bounce upward (support) or downward (resistance). Identifying these levels provides traders with key points for making market entry or exit decisions.
- **Indicators and Oscillators**: From simple moving averages to more complex tools like the MACD (Moving Average Convergence Divergence) or RSI (Relative Strength Index), indicators and oscillators offer additional insights into trend strength and potential reversal points, enriching analysis with quantitative data.

Application in Forex and Stock Markets

Technical analysis finds applications in both the Forex and stock markets, with some differences stemming from the nature of the assets and the structure of the markets themselves. In Forex, emphasis is placed on analyzing the movements of currency pairs in a 24-hour market. Tools such as candlestick charts and volatility indicators are particularly useful here.

In the stock market, technical analysis can be used to evaluate the performance of individual stocks or entire indices, focusing on price patterns and volumes within the specific trading hours of exchanges. With its pragmatic and visual approach, technical analysis provides traders with a lens to interpret the complexity of financial markets, offering a solid foundation for dynamic and informed trading strategies.

In the following sections, we will explore in detail how to leverage technical analysis tools and techniques to navigate successfully both the vibrant world of Forex and the rich diversity of the stock market.

Applications Beyond Forex and Stock Markets

While technical analysis is widely used in Forex and stock markets, its applicability extends far beyond these two domains. Markets such as commodities, cryptocurrencies, and even derivatives like futures and options are fertile grounds for applying technical analysis techniques. In each of these markets, the ability to read charts, interpret trading volumes, and use technical indicators allows traders to anticipate price movements and position themselves accordingly.

Here are some of the most important markets where technical analysis is widely used:

1. **Commodities Markets**: These include trading in natural resources such as oil, gold, silver, and other raw materials. Technical analysis helps forecast price movements of these commodities, which are influenced by factors such as political conditions, supply and demand changes, and shifts in global economic policies.
2. **Derivatives Markets**: Including financial instruments like options, futures, and swaps, whose prices are

derived from the value of other underlying assets (such as stocks, bonds, commodities, or indices). Technical analysis is used to identify trading opportunities and manage risk in these complex markets.
3. **Cryptocurrency Markets**: With the advent of cryptocurrencies like Bitcoin, Ethereum, and altcoins, technical analysis has become a key tool for navigating the volatility and unique trading patterns of these digital markets. Indicators such as moving averages, RSI, and chart patterns like triangles and head-and-shoulders are commonly used to analyze the cryptocurrency market.
4. **Debt Market (Bonds)**: While less common compared to stock or commodity markets, technical analysis can be applied to bond trading to identify price trends and trading opportunities based on interest rate movements and other economic factors.
5. **Real Estate Markets**: Although traditionally less associated with technical analysis, some investors use technical principles to evaluate trends and market cycles in real estate investments, particularly through REITs (Real Estate Investment Trusts) and other financial instruments linked to the real estate sector.

In each of these markets, technical analysis provides traders and investors with a framework to evaluate current market conditions, forecast future price movements, and make informed trading decisions. However, it is important to note that the effectiveness of technical analysis may vary depending on the specific market, and it should be used in conjunction with other forms of analysis and contextual considerations to optimize trading and investment strategies.

Technical analysis serves as a bridge between empirical observation of market data and the development of trading strategies grounded in quantitative and qualitative logic. Its value lies in its ability to synthesize vast amounts of data into manageable insights and to transform these insights into deliberate trading actions.

As financial markets continue to evolve and grow increasingly complex, technical analysis remains an indispensable tool for traders navigating the often turbulent waters of global trading.

In trading, reading charts is like deciphering the hidden language of the market. Support and resistance levels are among the most critical concepts in technical analysis, representing key points where an asset's price tends to pause, reverse direction, or consolidate. These levels not only help in understanding market dynamics but also serve as essential tools for making more informed trading decisions.

In the following sections, we will analyze chart examples to demonstrate how to identify and utilize support and resistance levels in different market scenarios. Each example is designed to help you grasp not only the theory but also how to apply it in the real world of trading.

This chart illustrates key concepts in technical analysis, focusing on **support, resistance**, and **breakout levels**. Here's how to interpret it:

1. **Support Levels**: These are marked where the price repeatedly found a lower boundary and rebounded upwards, typically observable near horizontal lines where multiple candles align their lows. Support levels indicate strong buying interest and are useful for predicting potential reversals during a downtrend.
2. **Resistance Levels**: Resistance zones are where the price consistently struggled to rise further, forming upper boundaries at similar high points across several candles. These levels highlight significant selling pressure that limits upward price movements.
3. **Break in Support**: A breakout below the support level occurs when the price falls decisively below a previously identified support zone. This event often signals the beginning of a new downtrend, marked by longer bearish candles.

104

This example provides a practical visualization of how price levels act as psychological barriers in the market. Observing these areas helps traders anticipate shifts in momentum and plan their trades effectively.

Understanding Trend Lines: The Foundation of Technical Analysis

Trend lines are one of the simplest yet most effective tools in technical analysis, serving as a visual representation of the market's direction. They help traders identify the overall trend and anticipate potential reversals or breakouts. A rising trend line, as depicted in the chart, connects a series of higher lows, showcasing a consistent upward momentum driven by strong buyer activity. However, no trend lasts forever. The breakdown of a trend line often signals a shift in market sentiment, where sellers begin to overpower buyers, potentially leading to a new downtrend. This transition is a critical moment for traders, providing both opportunities and risks.

The chart below highlights how a rising trend line forms and the significance of its eventual breakdown. By observing these patterns, traders can make more informed decisions, whether it's to enter a trade during the trend's continuation or to exit before a reversal. Understanding how to interpret and utilize trend lines is a cornerstone of any trader's journey toward mastering market dynamics.

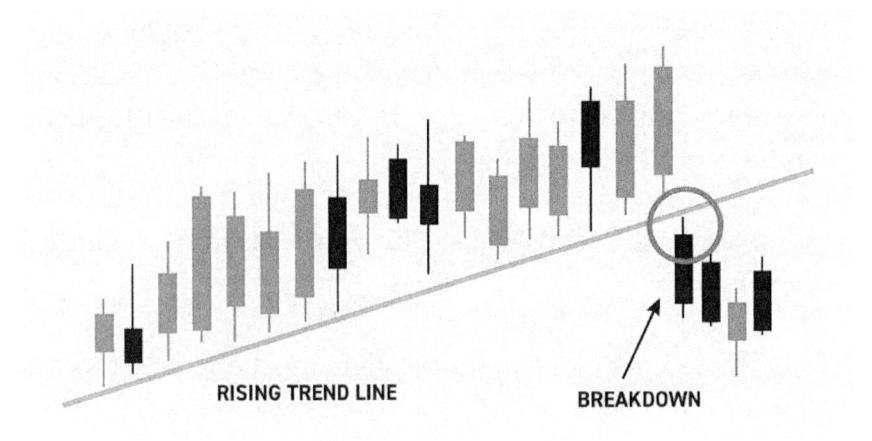

This chart illustrates the concept of a rising trend line and its subsequent breakdown, which is a key element of technical analysis. Trend lines are one of the most widely used tools by traders to identify and visualize the direction of the market. By connecting successive higher lows or lower highs, these lines provide a clear framework for interpreting price movements and anticipating potential shifts.

In this example, the rising trend line shows the consistent upward momentum of the market. Each candlestick touches or remains above the line, confirming the validity of the trend. However, the circled area highlights a critical moment when the price breaks below this trend line. This "breakdown" serves as an early warning that the upward momentum has weakened and may reverse into a downward trend.

Key Takeaways:

- **Trend Line Functionality:** A rising trend line connects multiple higher lows, acting as a dynamic

support level. When the price respects this line, it reinforces the strength of the trend.
- **Breakdown Significance:** A breakdown occurs when the price decisively closes below the trend line. This often signals a shift in market sentiment and the possibility of a new downward trend.
- **Practical Application:** Traders use trend lines and breakdowns to determine strategic entry or exit points. A breakdown could prompt selling or shorting, especially if confirmed by additional indicators or high trading volume.

By understanding the dynamics of trend lines and breakdowns, traders can enhance their ability to interpret market behavior and make more informed trading decisions.

Technical analysis is a cornerstone for anyone seeking to navigate financial markets with confidence. Through the use of charts, trends, support and resistance levels, indicators, and oscillators, this discipline transforms complex data into actionable insights that help traders make informed decisions. Above all, technical analysis teaches us to observe the market critically and recognize the hidden signals in price movements.

Its versatility makes it applicable to a wide range of financial instruments, from Forex to stocks, commodities, and cryptocurrencies. Each market has its own peculiarities, but the principles of technical analysis remain universal, providing a unique lens to interpret market dynamics and anticipate future developments.

However, it's important to remember that technical analysis should not be used in isolation. Context, the broader picture, and integration with other forms of analysis—such as fundamental analysis—are essential for building a robust and well-informed strategy. Even the most experienced traders rely on a combination of tools and methodologies to minimize risks and maximize opportunities.

Technical analysis, therefore, is not just a collection of tools but a mindset that encourages studying, understanding, and adapting to ever-changing markets. For beginner traders, it represents the first step toward greater awareness; for experienced ones, it is an indispensable companion. In all cases, its value lies in its ability to turn market uncertainty into concrete opportunities.

Fundamental Analysis: A Deep Dive into Financial Evaluation

Fundamental analysis stands as a cornerstone for investors aiming to build a long-term vision in the financial world. Unlike technical analysis, which focuses on price charts and trading patterns, fundamental analysis delves into the economic and financial "bones" of a company, sector, or even an entire nation's economy. This approach rests on the premise that the market price of a financial instrument may diverge from its intrinsic value due to various factors but will eventually tend to align with this fundamental value.

For long-term investors, understanding and applying fundamental analysis is essential. It provides a solid foundation for making well-informed investment decisions, enabling the identification of undervalued opportunities while steering clear of overpriced assets. In essence, fundamental analysis serves as a compass amidst a sea of financial data, guiding investors toward more strategic and insightful choices.

Deciphering Financial Statements

Financial statements act as a company's financial identity card, offering invaluable insights into its health and future prospects. Mastering these documents is a prerequisite for effective fundamental analysis.

The **Income Statement** provides a snapshot of a company's performance over a specific period, detailing revenue, costs, and net profit. Consistent revenue growth year-over-year reflects sustainable growth, while stable profit margins indicate efficient cost management.

The **Balance Sheet** paints a picture of a company's financial stability, presenting its assets and liabilities. A strong asset-to-liability ratio signals sound financial health, while excessive long-term debt may highlight potential risks.

The **Cash Flow Statement** details the inflow and outflow of cash, illustrating a company's liquidity. Healthy cash flow ensures a company can cover operational needs, invest in growth, and withstand economic downturns.

Understanding these key documents enables investors to assess a company's financial sustainability and growth potential.

Economic Indicators and Their Market Impact

Economic indicators act as the pulse of the global economy and have a direct influence on financial markets. Understanding these metrics is crucial for anticipating market moves.

GDP (Gross Domestic Product): This measures the total value of goods and services produced within a country and reflects overall economic health. Growing GDP signals economic expansion, which is typically favorable for companies and stock markets.

Interest Rates: Set by central banks, interest rates impact the cost of borrowing. Higher rates can curb consumer spending and investments, potentially slowing the economy, but they generally strengthen a currency's value in forex markets.

Inflation: The rise in consumer prices affects purchasing power and investment decisions. Moderate inflation is a normal sign of economic growth, but excessive or insufficient inflation can indicate underlying economic issues.

Analyzing the impact of these and other indicators on forex and stock markets helps investors predict market movements and uncover investment opportunities.

Evaluating Companies: The Core of Fundamental Analysis

At the heart of fundamental analysis lies the evaluation of companies using various methods and metrics to determine their intrinsic value.

The **P/E Ratio (Price to Earnings Ratio)** compares a company's current stock price to its earnings per share, providing a measure of relative valuation. A low P/E ratio may indicate undervaluation, though it must be assessed in the context of the industry and earnings growth.

The **P/B Ratio (Price to Book Ratio)** measures the market price of a stock against its book value per share. A ratio below 1 can suggest undervaluation, though this varies by sector.

ROE (Return on Equity) gauges how efficiently a company generates profits from shareholders' equity. A high ROE indicates effective use of capital to create earnings.

Analyzing these and other metrics lays a solid groundwork for informed investment decisions, identifying undervalued companies with strong growth prospects.

Fundamental analysis is more than just a set of tools—it's a philosophy for understanding markets on a deeper level. By combining financial statement analysis, macroeconomic insights, and company valuations, investors can develop a comprehensive strategy that balances risk and opportunity. Whether you're navigating the complexities of stocks, forex, or commodities, fundamental analysis equips you with the skills to invest with clarity and confidence.

Additional Aspects of Fundamental Analysis

Cash Flows and the Importance of Liquidity

A thorough fundamental analysis also requires a detailed examination of a company's cash flows, which represent its ability to generate liquidity. The Cash Flow Statement is divided into operating, investing, and financing activities, providing a comprehensive view of how the company generates and uses cash. Positive cash flow from operating activities is a strong indicator of financial health, demonstrating that the company can sustain itself through its core operations.

Economic Cycles and Industry Impact

Fundamental analysis must consider economic cycles and how they influence various sectors. Some companies, known as cyclical businesses, are heavily affected by general economic conditions, such as those in the automotive or construction sectors. Conversely, counter-cyclical companies tend to perform well even during recessions, such as those in essential goods or healthcare. Identifying a company's position within these cycles can provide valuable insights into its potential resilience or vulnerability.

Geopolitical and Regulatory Context

The geopolitical environment and regulatory framework can have significant impacts on a company's prospects. Events such as changes in trade policies, political tensions, or new environmental regulations can directly affect business operations and market opportunities. Analyzing these external factors is essential for assessing risks and opportunities that may not be evident from financial data alone.

Sustainability and Corporate Social Responsibility (CSR)

In today's context, sustainability and corporate social responsibility (CSR) are becoming increasingly important for investors. Companies adopting sustainable and ethical practices not only mitigate legal and reputational risks but can also leverage new market opportunities. Fundamental analysis should include an evaluation of how a company manages environmental, social, and governance (ESG) issues, as these can significantly influence long-term value.

The Complexity and Depth of Fundamental Analysis

Fundamental analysis is a multidimensional process that goes beyond simply reading financial data. It involves interpreting a wide range of factors, from financial solidity and operational performance to economic cycles, geopolitical context, and sustainability practices. Investors who master this art are better equipped to identify valuable investment opportunities while mitigating risks associated with market fluctuations. As such, fundamental analysis remains an indispensable tool in every serious investor's toolkit.

Case Studies in Fundamental Analysis

Case Study 1: Apple Inc.'s Turnaround

- **Context**: In the early 2000s, Apple Inc. began a transformation that turned it from a struggling company into a technological giant.
- **Fundamental Analysis Applied**: This included examining financial statements, revenue growth, profit margins, and product innovation with the introduction of the iPod, iPhone, and iPad.
- **Lessons Learned**: The importance of evaluating a company's ability to innovate and adapt, alongside the strength of its financial fundamentals.

Case Study 2: Volkswagen and the Dieselgate Scandal

- **Context**: In 2015, Volkswagen was involved in the "Dieselgate" scandal, which significantly impacted its market value.
- **Fundamental Analysis Applied**: Assessing the impact of legal sanctions, remediation costs, and the company's reputation on its financial fundamentals and stock price.
- **Lessons Learned**: The importance of considering ESG (Environmental, Social, and Governance) risks in fundamental analysis.

The Importance of Integrated Analysis in Trading and Investment

Relying solely on either technical or fundamental analysis can provide valuable insights but often fails to capture the entire picture. Technical analysis, focused on past prices and chart patterns, excels in identifying entry and exit points and understanding market psychology. On the other hand, fundamental analysis offers a robust understanding of an investment's intrinsic value by delving into economic, financial, and qualitative factors. Integrating these approaches allows investors to balance time horizons and risk perceptions, capitalizing on both short-term market trends and long-term value.

Benefits of Integrated Analysis

- **Balanced Decisions**: Integrated analysis enables investors to make balanced decisions that consider both current market contexts and an investment's fundamentals.
- **Improved Risk Management**: Combining the two analyses helps investors identify low-risk opportunities, leveraging technical trends while acknowledging fundamental realities.
- **Flexibility**: This approach offers greater adaptability, allowing investors to navigate a wide range of market scenarios and capitalize on diverse investment opportunities.

Application of Integrated Analysis: A Case Study

Imagine evaluating a tech company, "Tech Innovations Inc.," for a potential investment.

- **Fundamental Analysis**: Reveals strong financials, consistent revenue growth, high profit margins, and a solid balance sheet. The company also benefits from a leadership position in its sector, innovative products, and a robust R&D pipeline.
- **Technical Analysis**: Indicates that the stock is near a significant support level, with technical indicators suggesting a possible short-term upward reversal.

By integrating these analyses, an investor might conclude that "Tech Innovations Inc." represents not only a solid long-term investment but also a favorable short-term buying opportunity given the positive technical setup.

Integrated analysis is not just a compromise strategy; it's a holistic approach that enriches investors' understanding, enabling them to navigate financial markets with greater confidence and success. By combining the immediate insights of technical analysis with the in-depth valuation provided by fundamental analysis, investors can achieve a more comprehensive view and build more resilient and profitable portfolios over the long term.

Chapter 7: Trading Strategies

On the path to trading success, selecting and applying the right strategies is a pivotal step. This chapter serves as a compass, guiding traders through the broad spectrum of trading strategies available, equipping individuals of all levels with the knowledge needed to identify and implement those that align with their goals, lifestyles, and risk tolerance.

We will begin by exploring beginner-friendly strategies, such as trend trading and breakout trading, which rely on intuitive principles and require less intensive technical analysis. These strategies are excellent starting points for newcomers to the trading world, enabling them to build a solid understanding of market behavior while keeping things relatively simple.

As you gain confidence and experience, you can delve into strategies suited for intermediate traders, such as swing trading and scalping. These methods demand a deeper understanding of market movements and a greater commitment to active trading but can yield significant opportunities for those prepared to adapt quickly to changing market conditions.

We will also examine when and how to apply various strategies, considering market contexts, economic conditions, and other external factors that can influence the choice of the most appropriate approach. This section aims to empower you to dynamically adjust your trading approach in response to evolving market dynamics, thereby maximizing your chances of success.

Through this chapter, we aspire to provide a comprehensive and detailed overview of trading strategies, ranging from basic to advanced approaches. Whether you're just starting out or seeking to further refine your skills, this chapter offers the tools and insights needed to navigate the trading world with confidence and purpose.

Beginner Strategies: Trend Trading, Breakout Trading, and News Trading

In the dynamic world of trading, the right strategy can mean the difference between success and failure. This chapter begins with accessible strategies for beginners, such as trend trading, breakout trading, and news trading, before moving on to more sophisticated techniques like swing trading and scalping for those with some experience in financial markets.

News trading has been integrated into beginner strategies to highlight the importance of global dynamics and their impact on financial markets. This approach focuses on interpreting economic, political, and financial news and translating them into timely trading decisions. Whether it's economic announcements, central bank interest rate decisions, or geopolitical events, news trading requires quick thinking and a solid grasp of how these developments affect various assets.

Trend Trading is among the most popular and time-tested strategies for traders of all experience levels. Its core principle, "the trend is your friend," emphasizes the importance of aligning with the market's general direction to maximize profits and minimize risks.

Identifying Market Trends

Successfully identifying the market trend is the cornerstone of trend trading, which involves careful analysis of price charts and the use of technical tools:

- **Moving Averages**: Tools like the Simple Moving Average (SMA) or Exponential Moving Average (EMA) are commonly used. Observing the price relative to a moving average (e.g., 50-day or 200-day) offers clear indications of the prevailing trend. Generally, if the price is above the moving average, the trend is upward; if below, it's downward.
- **Trendlines**: Drawing trendlines that connect successive highs or lows on a chart provides a clear visual representation of market direction. A trendline breakout often signals a potential trend reversal.
- **Technical Indicators**: Indicators like the Average Directional Index (ADX) measure the strength of a

trend, offering additional insight for informed decision-making.

Entry Points

Timing is critical when entering a position in trend trading:

- **Trend Confirmation**: Traders should wait for confirmation that a trend is stable before entering. This can come from moving average crossovers or other technical indicators confirming the trend's direction and strength.
- **Pullbacks**: Temporary retracements against the main trend are often used as entry opportunities, targeting support or resistance areas where the price is likely to resume its original direction.

Risk Management

Effective risk management is essential for long-term success in trend trading:

- **Stop-Loss Orders**: Setting stop-loss orders just outside key support or resistance levels limits potential losses if the trend unexpectedly reverses. This strategy ensures traders exit losing positions before losses become significant.
- **Position Sizing**: Adjusting the position size based on trade risk and market volatility helps protect portfolio capital.
- **Active Monitoring**: Even strong trends can falter. Constant monitoring and a willingness to exit

positions if the trend shows signs of weakening are critical for minimizing losses.

In summary, trend trading relies on solid technical analysis and disciplined risk management. Traders adopting this strategy need patience, a commitment to trend confirmation, and adaptability to changing market conditions. With practice and experience, trend trading can become a powerful and profitable component of a broader trading strategy.

The concept of market structure is one of the fundamental pillars of technical analysis, essential for understanding price movements and identifying trading opportunities. This chart illustrates the three main types of trends that characterize financial markets: uptrend, downtrend, and sideways trend. Through a clear visual representation, the chart highlights how prices move in recurring patterns, marked by highs and lows that can be ascending, descending, or stable.

Let us now delve into each component of market structure to understand how these elements can guide trading decisions.

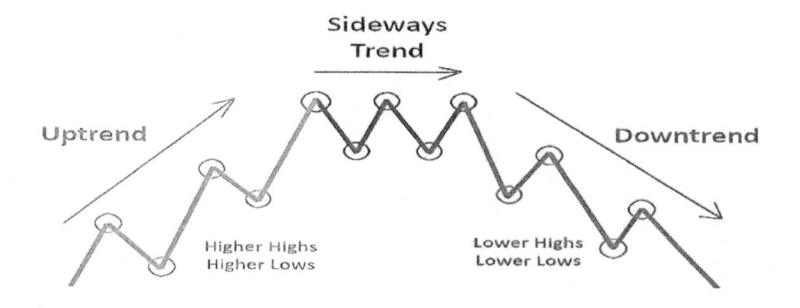

The market structure chart provides a clear and schematic representation of the three main price movements: uptrend, downtrend, and sideways trend. Each section of the chart reflects specific market behavior and offers valuable insights for traders.

Uptrend: An uptrend occurs when prices display a sequence of higher highs and higher lows. This movement indicates a dominance of buyers in the market, suggesting that prices will continue to rise. In the chart, the points where prices reach new highs and return to higher levels than the previous low are defined as "higher highs" and "higher lows." These signals are crucial for traders seeking buying opportunities.

Sideways Trend: A sideways trend represents a consolidation phase where prices move within a defined range without a clear direction upward or downward. This type of movement indicates a balance between buyers and sellers, often associated with a period of market indecision. Traders can exploit these ranges with range trading strategies, buying at support levels and selling at resistance levels.

Downtrend: A downtrend occurs when prices display a sequence of lower highs and lower lows. This movement signals a dominance of sellers, suggesting that prices will continue to decline. In the chart, the points where prices reach new lows and return to lower levels than the previous high are defined as "lower highs" and "lower lows." These signals are useful for traders seeking selling opportunities.

Trend trading within the market structure offers a solid and intuitive strategy for traders who aim to align themselves with the prevailing price movement. As the famous mantra "the trend is your friend" suggests, identifying and following upward or downward trends allows traders to maximize profits by leveraging market momentum.

Even during sideways phases, the ability to interpret the overall structure helps pinpoint potential breakout or breakdown points, providing targeted trading opportunities. However, the primary focus remains on recognizing the dominant direction and acting with discipline and consistency.

Following the trend is not just a strategy but a fundamental principle that reduces uncertainty and improves the likelihood of success over time. In an ever-evolving market, staying in tune with prevailing trends enables traders to navigate with greater confidence, turning market changes into growth opportunities.

Breakout Trading

Breakout trading is a strategy designed to capitalize on moments when the price of an asset surpasses a specific resistance or support level, signaling the potential start of a new trend. These significant price movements, or "breakouts," often occur following periods of consolidation or within specific chart patterns. They present trading opportunities as they are typically followed by rapid and directional price movements.

Identifying Breakouts

The success of breakout trading begins with the ability to accurately identify price patterns that indicate a potential breakout. These include:

- **Chart Patterns**: Triangles (ascending, descending, and symmetrical), rectangles, and head-and-shoulders formations are among the most common patterns traders monitor for breakouts. These patterns reflect consolidation phases that often precede significant price movements.
- **Support and Resistance Levels**: Breakouts occur when the price surpasses resistance levels (in an uptrend) or falls below support levels (in a downtrend). Identifying these key levels through historical price analysis is essential for anticipating potential breakouts.
- **Volume**: An increase in trading volume during a breakout is often considered confirmation of the movement's strength, enhancing the likelihood of the new trend's continuation.

Entry Points

Timing is everything in breakout trading. Determining the optimal moment to enter a trade requires precision:

- **Breakout Confirmation**: Traders wait for a candlestick to close outside the consolidation pattern or beyond the resistance/support level to confirm the breakout's validity. Entering too early can expose

traders to the risk of false breakouts, while entering too late may reduce profit potential.
- **Entry Strategies**: Some traders prefer to enter immediately after the breakout confirmation, while others might wait for a pullback or retracement to the breakout level before entering, aiming for a better risk/reward ratio.

Risk Management

Risk management is critical in breakout trading due to the speed and volatility often associated with these movements:

- **Stop-Loss**: Placing stop-loss orders slightly beyond the breakout point can help protect against sudden reversals and limit losses. The stop-loss distance may vary depending on the asset's volatility and individual risk preferences.
- **Risk/Reward Assessment**: Before entering a trade, it's crucial to evaluate the potential risk/reward ratio, ensuring that the position size and stop-loss align with the trader's overall risk management strategy.

When executed correctly, breakout trading can offer significant profit opportunities. However, it requires discipline, thorough technical analysis, and robust risk management. Traders who master these skills can use breakout trading as an effective strategy to capitalize on market movements.

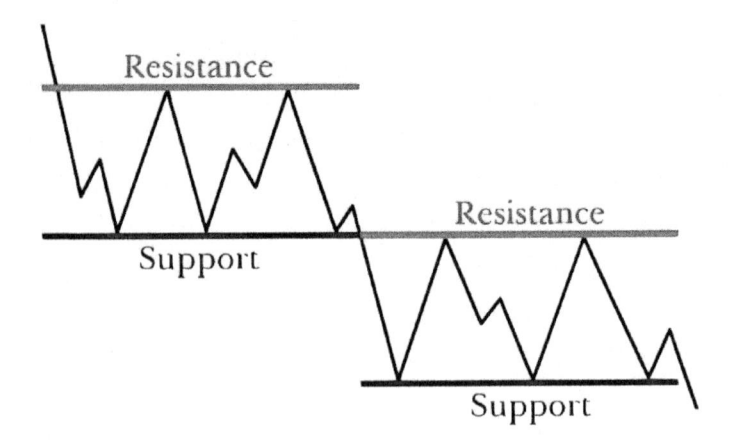

This chart clearly illustrates the concept of **breakout trading**, a central aspect of technical analysis. The **support** levels (lower line) and **resistance** levels (upper line) represent key zones where the price tends to bounce or face difficulty breaking through. In the chart, you can observe price movements within these two levels, indicating a period of market consolidation.

The **breakout** occurs when the price surpasses the resistance level (upward movement) or breaks below the support level (downward movement). This breakthrough signifies a significant shift in market dynamics, often accompanied by an increase in trading volume, confirming the strength of the movement.

- **Bullish breakout**: When the price breaks above the resistance level, it may indicate the beginning of an upward trend.

- **Bearish breakout**: When the price breaks below the support level, it may signal the start of a downward trend.

To correctly interpret a breakout, it's important to consider the overall market context and confirm the movement with additional technical indicators, such as volume or candlestick patterns.

Breakout trading, as shown in this chart, offers unique opportunities to capitalize on significant changes in price movements. However, it's essential to remember that not all breakouts lead to sustained trends. **False breakouts**, where the price quickly returns within the consolidation levels, pose a risk that must be managed with a well-defined **stop-loss strategy** and careful technical analysis.

In conclusion, this approach requires discipline, patience, and the ability to recognize key signals in the market. With experience, breakout trading can become a powerful and reliable component of any trader's toolkit, offering profit opportunities in volatile and dynamic markets.

News Trading

News trading involves opening positions in response to significant economic news or corporate announcements that have the potential to move markets. Events such as interest rate decisions, employment reports, quarterly earnings results, and other economic indicators can create immediate trading opportunities due to market reactions to these developments.

Preparation and research are essential for success in news trading. Staying informed about upcoming news events by consulting economic calendars and following reliable financial news sources is a key part of this strategy. Understanding the potential impact of certain news on markets or specific sectors and stocks is equally important. For example, an interest rate hike might negatively affect real estate stocks, while strong employment data might boost market sentiment.

Timing is critical, and planning entry and exit points in advance can help traders navigate the volatility that often accompanies news releases. Some traders position themselves just before the announcement, aiming to capitalize on anticipated movements, while others prefer to wait for the initial market reaction to subside to avoid the immediate fluctuations. Managing risk is also a fundamental aspect of news trading. Given the potential for rapid and unpredictable market movements, employing strategies such as stop-loss orders can protect capital from significant losses.

News trading demands the ability to quickly assess information and act decisively, as markets can respond almost instantaneously to major announcements. This strategy is particularly appealing to traders who actively follow global and economic events and can interpret how these developments impact various financial assets.

In summary, news trading and trend trading together form a strong foundation of strategies for beginners venturing into the world of trading. Each strategy has its unique advantages and is suitable for different markets and conditions. Understanding the principles of these strategies and practicing effective risk management are essential steps in building a solid trading foundation.

Strategies for Intermediates: Swing Trading, Scalping and Day Trading

Swing trading is rooted in the natural desire to capitalize on the market's inherent price fluctuations. This strategy focuses on significant price movements that occur over a few days or weeks, rather than minute-by-minute changes typical of day trading.

Historically, swing trading has always been a core approach in financial markets. Before the advent of digital trading, market participants relied on daily bar charts and price curves to identify trends and opportunities. As technology evolved, traders gained access to real-time data and advanced charting tools, enabling them to better identify market trends and turning points.

The philosophy behind swing trading assumes that market prices follow predictable cycles of upward and downward movements. Swing traders leverage technical analysis to spot these cycles and determine the points where the market is likely to shift direction. Instead of chasing immediate gains, they aim for more substantial profits by riding the wave of a trend over an extended period.

Who Uses Swing Trading?

Swing trading is favored by individual traders and fund managers looking to outperform the market without the continuous engagement required for day trading. This approach appeals particularly to those balancing other commitments, as it allows them to trade around their lifestyle rather than adapt their life to the demands of trading.

Swing trading is most effective in markets that exhibit clear directional trends but are not excessively volatile. In highly volatile or sideways markets, identifying and following consistent price movements becomes more challenging. Successful swing traders often combine their technical analysis skills with a broad understanding of macroeconomic conditions to improve their decision-making.

Timing is crucial in swing trading. Key market activity periods, such as market openings, closings, or the release of major economic data, often present the best opportunities. Experienced traders understand that timing the market is more critical than simply spending time in the market. Swing trading focuses on being present at the right time to capture significant moves.

In essence, swing trading is a tactical approach suited for those who prefer a measured, reflective engagement with the financial markets, taking advantage of the market's natural rhythms to achieve consistent success.

Characteristics of Swing Trading

For swing traders, selecting the right assets is an art requiring discernment and a deep understanding of market dynamics. They seek assets that display not only strong trends and volatility but also sufficient liquidity, ensuring smooth entry and exit from positions. Preference is often given to stocks or instruments that exhibit predictable patterns or respond to specific market triggers.

Technical analysis serves as the compass guiding swing traders through often unpredictable markets. Using tools like moving averages to identify trends, RSI (Relative Strength Index) to assess momentum, and patterns such as triangles or flags to forecast future movements, swing traders develop a nuanced understanding of price action.

Risk management is another cornerstone of swing trading. Traders employ strategies such as setting stop-loss levels to cap potential losses, planning take-profit levels to secure gains when targets are reached, and optimizing position sizing based on the risk level of each trade.

The successful execution of swing trading requires identifying trends, defining optimal entry and exit points based on technical indicators and support/resistance levels, monitoring broader market conditions, and adhering to a disciplined trading plan. Discipline is critical to avoid impulsive decisions and to follow a carefully considered strategy, even when emotional challenges arise during trading.

Swing trading, therefore, offers a dynamic and thoughtful way for traders to engage with the markets, enabling them to capitalize on its natural rhythms while maintaining a balanced and calculated approach.

Scalping

Scalping is one of the oldest trading strategies, rooted in the simple premise that frequent small profits can accumulate rapidly. Initially practiced on the trading floors of stock exchanges, scalping involved traders exploiting small price movements during the day.

With the advent of computers and internet access, scalping has evolved into a more accessible and sophisticated practice. The introduction of electronic trading enabled scalpers to use online platforms to execute a high volume of low-margin trades quickly. This approach perfectly aligns with the digital era, where many scalpers rely on algorithms and automated systems to enhance efficiency.

Scalping is well-suited for traders who can dedicate their full attention to the market throughout the trading session. It demands exceptional discipline, impeccable emotional control, and the ability to make quick and consistent decisions. While it is not suitable for everyone, those who master it can find it highly rewarding. Scalping is most effective in liquid markets with good volatility, where small price movements occur frequently and predictably.

Scalpers often capitalize on market events such as the opening and closing of exchanges or the release of economic data, where volatility and volume can spike. Timing is crucial for a scalper. These traders operate on very short timeframes, such as one- or five-minute charts, and may hold positions for mere seconds or a few minutes. The goal is to seize market opportunities and exit quickly once a small profit is achieved.

Scalping requires a significant investment of time, attention, and resources. For many, it is an intense trading style that combines technical analysis, risk management, and a robust trading infrastructure. With the rise of high-frequency trading (HFT) and trading bots, scalping has reached new levels of competition. However, for traders who can dedicate the necessary focus and possess the required discipline, scalping remains a highly attractive strategy.

Depth of Scalping

Scalping is a high-frequency trading strategy tailored for fast-paced market environments and relies on rapid execution of trades. This approach is built on repeatedly securing small profits throughout the trading day via numerous transactions.

The essence of scalping lies in its high trading frequency. Scalpers focus on exploiting the smallest, most frequent price movements rather than aiming for large market shifts.

Scalpers may execute dozens or even hundreds of trades within a single trading session. Each trade targets a minimal profit, often a few cents or fractions of a percentage point.

Real-Time Market Analysis

Scalping demands intensive real-time market analysis. Traders must interpret market data swiftly and act accordingly. Advanced trading systems are crucial, as scalpers rely on ultra-low latency platforms capable of near-instantaneous order execution. They also utilize technical indicators such as the Volume Weighted Average Price (VWAP) and Moving Average Convergence Divergence (MACD) to make fast and informed decisions.

Time Management and Continuous Focus

The core of scalping lies in the trader's ability to remain focused and responsive throughout the trading session. Scalping is often a full-time activity that requires the trader's undivided attention. Continuous monitoring of the markets is necessary to seize trading opportunities as soon as they arise.

Implementing Scalping Successfully

A well-defined trading plan is essential for successful scalping. Rapid entry and exit strategies are critical, with scalpers establishing precise rules for positions based on specific technical signals or risk management criteria. Emotional control is vital, as the speed and volume of trades leave no room for emotional overwhelm. Additionally, choosing brokers with low commissions and tight spreads is imperative to minimize the impact of transaction costs on profits.

Ultimately, scalping is a trading strategy that requires a unique blend of sophisticated technical tools, quick reflexes, iron discipline, and a well-calibrated risk tolerance. This strategy is ideal for those who thrive in high-paced trading environments and can handle the pressure of constant, rapid decision-making.

The table below compares two of the most popular trading strategies: Swing Trading and Scalping. While these methodologies share some fundamental principles, they differ significantly in approach, timing, and objectives. The choice between Swing Trading and Scalping largely depends on your trading style, risk tolerance, and the time you can dedicate to monitoring the market. By analyzing this comparison, it will be easier to understand which strategy best suits your needs and trader profile.

Aspect	Swing Trading	Scalping
Objective	Capture medium-term price swings over days or weeks	Capture small, frequent profits from rapid price movements
Time Commitment	Moderate (hours per day)	High (constant monitoring during trading hours)
Position Holding	Hours to weeks	Seconds to minutes
Tools	Charts, RSI, Moving Averages	VWAP, MACD, Low-latency platforms
Risk Management	Stop-loss, risk/reward assessment	Strict stop-loss, low capital exposure per trade
Market Environment	Trending or moderately volatile markets	Highly liquid and volatile markets
Ideal for	Traders with limited time, seeking larger profit margins	Traders who can focus intensely and handle stress

When and How to Apply Trading Strategies for Beginners

In the dynamic world of trading, understanding when and how to apply various strategies is essential for successfully navigating financial markets. For beginners, choosing the right strategy depends on several factors, including risk tolerance, investment goals, and the time available to dedicate to trading.

Trend trading is ideal in a market that shows a clear direction, whether upward or downward. Patience is key: you must wait for the right moment to enter, which occurs when technical signals confirm that the trend is strong and stable. This strategy works best during periods of economic stability, where external events have less influence on market movements. Beginners should focus on markets or securities known for their predictable patterns while avoiding overly volatile or unpredictable ones.

Breakout trading is well-suited to situations where the market is consolidating or when significant economic announcements are expected to push prices beyond a well-established support or resistance level. Acting quickly once the breakout is confirmed is crucial, along with setting appropriate stop-loss orders to protect against false signals. This strategy is particularly effective when there are indications of significant changes in market sentiment or a company's fundamentals.

Finally, news trading involves taking positions based on price fluctuations caused by important news events. It's essential to have a solid understanding of how specific news items can impact markets and act accordingly. This style of trading requires staying updated on current events and quickly interpreting how these events affect various financial assets. Beginners should approach news trading cautiously, starting with more predictable events with clear impacts.

In all cases, beginners must start with proper education and practice in a simulated trading environment before moving to real capital operations. Continuous practice and studying market dynamics are essential for developing the intuition and skills necessary for successful trading.

When and How to Apply Trading Strategies for Intermediates

As traders progress in their journey, they face the task of refining their craft, honing strategies, and learning to interpret the market not just through its numbers but through the stories those numbers tell. This level of trading goes beyond understanding the basics and requires deeper immersion into the complexities of the market and the nuances of various strategies.

Whether it's swing trading or scalping, each approach requires detailed knowledge and precise application to be effective. Swing trading is a medium-term strategy that suits those who cannot dedicate every single minute to market screens but still have enough time to plan and carefully monitor their positions. Unlike day trading, which demands constant attention to intraday charts, swing trading allows for decision-making over a longer timeframe. Traders can analyze market movements at the end of the day or week to make informed decisions.

Swing trading offers an opportunity to capitalize on price fluctuations without needing to react to every minor variation. However, it requires a solid understanding of when and how to enter and exit the market. The key lies in identifying medium-term trends and recognizing price patterns that signal the beginning or end of a market move.

Applying swing trading begins with diligent research. Traders must develop a hypothesis based on technical and fundamental analysis and set rigorous criteria for entry and exit. This might include waiting for trend confirmation through a recognized price pattern or using technical indicators to pinpoint an optimal entry point.

Scalping, on the other hand, is the polar opposite of swing trading in terms of timeframe. It's an art requiring a combination of speed, discipline, and emotional control. Scalpers thrive on the adrenaline of fast markets and can handle numerous transactions, profiting from small price movements throughout the day.

To successfully implement scalping, traders must ensure access to a trading platform capable of quickly processing high volumes of orders and providing real-time market data. The entry and exit strategy must be executed with surgical precision; scalpers must predefine their profit targets for each trade and adhere to them without hesitation.

A deep understanding of risk management is crucial in scalping. Since the strategy relies on marginal gains, a single loss can wipe out multiple small profits. Therefore, scalpers must use strict stop-loss orders and avoid letting losses outweigh accumulated gains. Both swing trading and scalping demand a mindset and approach that go beyond merely recognizing patterns.

Intermediate traders must develop an intuition for the market, understand the mass psychology that drives prices, and remain committed to their strategy even when the market appears to move against them. This level of trading isn't just about following rules; it's about understanding, adapting, and ultimately internalizing them. With practice, patience, and perseverance, intermediate traders can navigate markets successfully, leveraging their experience to seize trading opportunities that elude those who stop at the beginner level.

Day Trading: Navigating Real-Time Markets

Day trading is one of the most dynamic and fast-paced trading strategies, where positions are opened and closed within the same trading day. This approach eliminates the risks associated with overnight positions, such as price gaps and unexpected news, but requires constant attention and quick decision-making to capitalize on short-term market movements. Popular in markets like stocks, forex, and cryptocurrencies, day trading thrives on intraday volatility, creating numerous opportunities for profit.

Day trading stands apart from other strategies, such as swing trading or scalping, due to its focus on intraday operations and the necessity for traders to adapt to real-time market changes. It demands a disciplined approach and sharp analytical skills to identify entry and exit points effectively.

Key Components of Day Trading

To succeed in day trading, a comprehensive understanding of its tools, techniques, and psychological demands is crucial:

1. **Advanced Tools for Analysis**: Day traders rely heavily on detailed intraday charts with intervals as short as 1, 5, or 15 minutes. Indicators such as the Volume Weighted Average Price (VWAP), Moving Averages, and the Relative Strength Index (RSI) are commonly used to gauge price trends and momentum. Access to real-time data and fast execution platforms is essential to keep pace with the rapid fluctuations of intraday markets.
2. **Core Strategies in Day Trading**:
    - **Momentum Trading**: This approach focuses on exploiting rapid price movements triggered by news events, earnings reports, or significant increases in trading volume. Momentum traders aim to "ride the wave" of these sharp price shifts.
    - **Gap Trading**: Day traders often target price gaps that occur at market open due to overnight news or pre-market activity. By

analyzing the direction and strength of these gaps, they can position themselves to take advantage of the subsequent movement.
    - **Intraday Breakouts**: Identifying and trading on breakouts above resistance levels or below support levels during the trading day is a hallmark of successful day trading. These moves are often accompanied by increased volume, signaling strong market sentiment.
3. **Risk Management and Position Sizing**: Effective risk management is the cornerstone of day trading. Traders set tight stop-loss levels to limit potential losses and establish a clear risk/reward ratio for each trade. Position sizing is carefully calculated based on the volatility of the asset and the trader's risk tolerance.
4. **Psychological Resilience**: The rapid pace and high volume of trades in day trading require exceptional mental discipline and focus. Emotional control is paramount, as impulsive decisions driven by fear or greed can quickly erode profits. Successful day traders develop the ability to stay calm under pressure and adhere strictly to their trading plan.

The Ideal Day Trader

Day trading is best suited for individuals who can dedicate significant time and energy to actively monitoring the markets throughout the day. It requires a full-time commitment, a high level of expertise, and the ability to thrive in high-pressure environments. Traders with a passion for analyzing short-term price movements and a willingness to engage in frequent trades may find day trading particularly rewarding.

Day Trading in Action

Day trading often involves leveraging advanced technology to gain an edge. High-speed internet, low-latency platforms, and access to live news feeds are critical components of a day trader's toolkit. Many day traders also utilize algorithmic trading or automated systems to execute trades with precision, reducing the risk of human error.

For example, a day trader monitoring the release of a key economic indicator like non-farm payrolls may prepare to act immediately as the data hits the market. By analyzing how similar announcements have impacted price movements in the past, the trader can make an informed decision and execute trades in seconds, capitalizing on the heightened volatility.

Challenges and Rewards

While day trading offers the potential for significant profits, it is not without challenges. The need for constant vigilance, the pressure of quick decision-making, and the potential for losses can make it a demanding pursuit. However, for those who develop the necessary skills and discipline, day trading can be both lucrative and intellectually stimulating.

Day trading is a high-stakes, high-reward strategy that requires a unique combination of technical expertise, emotional control, and a disciplined approach to risk management. It offers an exciting opportunity for traders willing to dedicate the time and effort needed to master its complexities. By combining real-time market analysis with well-defined strategies, day traders can navigate the fast-moving financial landscape with confidence and precision.

Chapter 8: Risk Management

Risk management is one of the fundamental pillars for anyone venturing into the world of trading. Financial markets, by their very nature, are influenced by a wide array of factors, many of which lie beyond a trader's control. Global events, changes in economic policies, imbalances in supply and demand, and even geopolitical shifts can lead to sudden and unpredictable price swings. In such a volatile landscape, the ability to manage risk becomes an indispensable tool for protecting capital and ensuring the sustainability of trading activities.

Approaching trading without a risk management strategy is akin to navigating stormy seas without a compass. Even the most skilled and technically proficient traders can suffer significant losses if they fail to adopt a systematic approach to limit exposure to risk. Risk management is not merely an option—it is an essential requirement for surviving and thriving in the trading world. It enables traders to safeguard their capital, the single most important resource for any trader, and lays the foundation for achieving consistent and sustainable results over time.

The primary goal of risk management is to protect capital. To remain active in the markets, a trader must avoid significant portfolio damage, regardless of how promising a trading opportunity may appear. Effective risk management not only prevents catastrophic losses but also contributes to the consistency of results. This stability allows traders to maintain psychological and emotional balance, reducing stress and fostering more rational and deliberate decision-making.

Risk management is a structured process built upon several core principles. First and foremost, a trader must have a clear understanding of their own risk tolerance. Knowing how much one is willing to risk and what level of loss is bearable helps establish precise limits for every trade. Additionally, risk management decisions should be data-driven and informed by analysis. Examining historical market behavior and using probabilistic tools can help identify potential scenarios and prepare accordingly. Finally, having a well-defined plan is critical—it should include detailed rules on when to enter and exit trades, how to size positions, and how to respond to unexpected events.

Despite thorough preparation, risk management does not eliminate the possibility of losses entirely. Trading remains an inherently uncertain activity, and every trader must accept that losses are an inevitable part of the process. However, risk management provides a crucial defense against uncontrolled losses and allows traders to maximize their chances of long-term success. It serves as a framework of control, enabling traders to navigate the pitfalls of the market without being overwhelmed by volatility.

Ultimately, risk management is more than just a technique — it is a mindset, a strategic approach that transforms uncertainty into a manageable variable. Through careful planning and the use of appropriate tools, traders not only protect their capital but also lay the groundwork for a successful career in trading. Managing risk effectively is the first step toward sustainability and growth in the long term, ensuring that traders can weather the challenges of the markets and capitalize on opportunities with confidence.

Matplotlib Chart

Trade	Total Capital	% Risk per Trade	Capital at Risk	Entry Price	Stop Loss	Position Size
1	$10,000	2%	$200	$50	$45	40 shares
2	$10,000	2%	$200	$100	$90	20 shares
3	$10,000	2%	$200	$25	$22	80 shares

Note: The position size is calculated to ensure that the loss does not exceed the capital at risk if the price reaches the stop loss level.

Case Study: Risk Management in Action

Scenario: Maria is a trader who strictly follows risk management rules. She decides never to risk more than 2% of her $10,000 capital on a single trade.

Trade 1: Maria identifies a trading opportunity in a tech company. The stock price is $50, and her analysis suggests a stop loss at $45. Based on her 2% rule, Maria calculates that she can risk $200 on this trade. To determine the position size, she divides the capital at risk by the difference between the entry price and the stop loss ($50 - $45 = $5), arriving at a position size of 40 shares.

Outcome: After a few days, the price drops to $45, triggering Maria's stop loss. Her loss is $200, exactly 2% of her capital, as planned.

Reflection: Although Maria incurred a loss, her risk management strategy worked as intended, protecting most of her capital from a larger loss. Thanks to her discipline, she is ready to seek the next trading opportunity.

This case study demonstrates how effective risk management can safeguard a trader from excessive losses, allowing them to continue trading even after an unsuccessful trade.

How to Calculate Risk and Position Sizing

Determining the risk per trade is crucial for surviving and thriving in the dynamic world of trading. By using a fixed percentage of your total capital, such as 1–2%, you can limit potential losses and protect your portfolio from sudden shocks. This practice not only preserves capital but also promotes consistency in trading results, allowing you to stay in the game even after a streak of consecutive losses.

When deciding on the percentage of risk per trade, it's essential to consider your risk tolerance, financial goals, and capital size. A trader with substantial capital and a low risk tolerance might opt for a more conservative percentage, while someone with modest capital and a higher risk appetite could choose to risk a slightly larger percentage.

Limiting risk for each trade helps control losses, ensuring they don't significantly erode your capital. Furthermore, establishing a fixed risk per trade contributes to more consistent trading outcomes and improves emotional management during trades. Knowing your risk limit per trade also guides you in selecting stop-loss levels, a critical component of an effective exit strategy.

Practical Example

Let's consider Marco, a trader with $10,000 in capital. By deciding to risk 2% of his capital on each trade, Marco ensures that he doesn't risk more than $200 per trade. This approach allows him to preserve his capital, keeping losses within a manageable fraction of his portfolio.

Suppose Marco identifies a trading opportunity and, based on his analysis, sets a stop loss that would result in a $200 loss if triggered. By dividing the capital at risk ($200) by the difference between the entry price and the stop-loss level, Marco can calculate the optimal position size for that specific trade.

Establishing and adhering to a precise risk per trade is a non-negotiable practice for anyone aspiring to trade successfully. This limit not only serves to protect your capital but also acts as a safeguard against emotional decisions, which are often the cause of significant losses. As a trader, your primary goal is survival; only by preserving your capital can you seize the numerous opportunities the market has to offer.

Position Sizing Calculation

Determining the optimal position size is a crucial step in effectively managing risk. This process helps you determine how many units of an asset to buy or sell while adhering to your acceptable level of risk.

Simple Formula for Calculation:

Position Size = Capital at Risk / (Entry Price - Stop Loss)

- **Capital at Risk:** The amount of money you are willing to lose on a single trade.
- **Entry Price:** The price at which you plan to enter the market.
- **Stop Loss:** The price level at which you decide to exit the position to limit your losses.

Example 1: Stock Trading

- **Giulia's Capital:** $20,000
- **Risk per Trade:** 1%
- **Capital at Risk:** $200 ($20,000 x 1%)
- **Entry Price:** $100
- **Stop Loss:** $95

Calculation:
Position Size = $200 / ($100 - $95) = 40 shares
Giulia should purchase 40 shares for this trade.

Example 2: Forex Trading

- **Marco's Capital:** $30,000
- **Risk per Trade:** 2%
- **Capital at Risk:** $600
- **Entry Price:** 1.1200 (EUR/USD)
- **Stop Loss:** 1.1150

Calculation:
Position Size = $600 / (1.1200 - 1.1150) = 12,000 units
Marco should trade 12,000 units of EUR/USD.

Example 3: Cryptocurrency Trading

- **Sofia's Capital:** $15,000
- **Risk per Trade:** 1.5%
- **Capital at Risk:** $225
- **Entry Price:** $250
- **Stop Loss:** $240

Calculation:
Position Size = $225 / ($250 - $240) = 22.5 units
Sofia should purchase approximately 22.5 units of Bitcoin.

Position sizing calculations are essential for keeping losses within acceptable limits and preserving capital over the long term. By adopting this methodical approach, you can trade with greater confidence and ensure your capital remains intact for future trading opportunities.

Example Chart for Risk Management in Trading

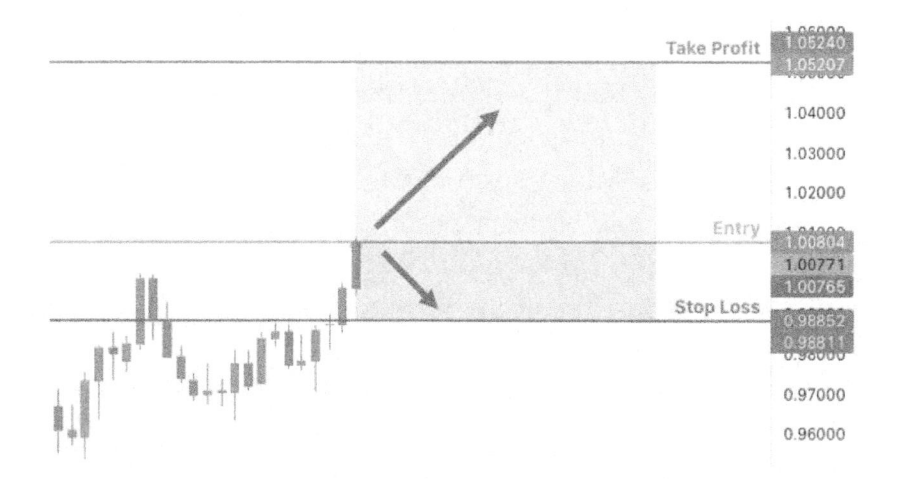

The chart serves as an excellent visual example to illustrate the relationship between the entry price, stop loss, and take profit in a trading operation.

Here are some key points you can emphasize when including it in your book:

1. **Entry Point**: This is the price level where the trader enters the market. The chart clearly highlights this point, which is essential for calculating both risk and position size.
2. **Stop Loss**: This indicates the price level where the trader chooses to exit in order to minimize losses if the market moves against their position. On the chart, this

threshold is clearly marked and helps establish the maximum amount the trader is willing to lose.
3. **Take Profit**: This represents the price level at which the trader plans to exit the market to secure a profit. This is also clearly shown on the chart and helps define the trader's profit objective for the position.
4. **Position Sizing**: While the chart doesn't directly show how to calculate position size, it provides the necessary information to do so. You can explain that, by knowing the entry point and stop loss, a trader can use the formula you provided to calculate the appropriate position size to keep the risk within established limits.
5. **Risk/Reward Ratio**: The chart also helps visualize the risk/reward ratio, which is the distance between the entry point and the stop loss compared to the distance between the entry point and the take profit. This ratio is crucial for assessing whether a trade is worth pursuing.

Market Considerations and Asset Types

Risk calculation and position sizing are crucial components of risk management in trading, but there is no one-size-fits-all approach that applies to every market or asset type. Market conditions and the inherent characteristics of assets demand tailored risk management strategies.

Here's how these variables influence risk calculation and position sizing, along with insights on how to adapt your approach effectively.

Volatility, which measures the magnitude of price fluctuations over time, is a key factor in risk calculation. The higher the volatility, the greater the price swings, and consequently, the higher the risk of unexpected losses. In highly volatile markets, such as cryptocurrencies, it may be prudent to reduce the risk per trade—perhaps risking only 1% of capital instead of 2%—to account for the larger price movements. Conversely, in less volatile markets like bonds, you might allow for slightly higher risk per trade, given the relatively stable price variations.

The type of asset being traded also significantly impacts position sizing. Stocks, forex, and cryptocurrencies each exhibit varying levels of liquidity, volatility, and minimum position sizes, all of which must be factored into the calculation. Stocks often present variable liquidity and volatility; for highly liquid stocks, you might use standard position sizes, whereas for less liquid or more volatile ones, a smaller position might be safer.

Forex markets, known for their high liquidity and leverage availability, require careful position sizing to ensure leverage does not inflate risk beyond acceptable limits. Cryptocurrencies, being notoriously volatile, may necessitate conservative position sizes and wider stop-loss levels to accommodate their sharp price swings without being prematurely stopped out.

To adapt your risk management strategy to market conditions and asset types, consider the following steps:

First, assess the volatility of the asset using tools like the Average True Range (ATR) and adjust your risk per trade and stop-loss levels accordingly. In leveraged markets like forex, tailor position sizes to ensure leverage does not magnify risk beyond acceptable thresholds. Monitor market events, such as economic announcements or data releases, which can spike volatility, and consider reducing position sizes or using wider stop-loss levels during these times. Customize stop-loss levels based on factors like historical volatility and your personal risk tolerance to align with the specific market and asset conditions.

Additionally, continually review and adjust your risk management practices. Markets are constantly evolving, and your strategy should adapt to reflect new information and changing conditions. Risk management is not a "set it and forget it" strategy—it's a dynamic process requiring ongoing attention and fine-tuning.

By implementing these principles, you can navigate various markets and asset types with greater confidence and potentially enhance your long-term trading performance.

Chapter 9: Leverage

Leverage is one of the most fascinating and risky tools in the world of trading and investments. Its ability to multiply market exposure using only a fraction of one's own capital makes it an incredibly powerful resource for traders. However, this very characteristic also makes it a double-edged sword, capable of amplifying not only gains but also losses.

In simple terms, leverage allows traders to control large positions by investing a relatively small amount of their own capital, known as "margin." This feature significantly enhances the potential return on investment but also introduces a proportionally higher level of risk. Leverage is commonly expressed as a ratio, such as 10:1, meaning that with one dollar of personal capital, a trader can control positions worth ten dollars. While this opportunity may seem attractive, the downside is that losses can easily exceed the initial investment, requiring careful and informed management.

The concept of leverage has its roots in centuries past, originally associated with financing long-distance commercial ventures. Over time, its application has evolved to encompass modern financial markets.

With the development of stock exchanges and technological advancements, leverage has become an essential tool for trading stocks, bonds, currencies, and derivatives. The advent of online trading has further expanded access to leverage, enabling a broad range of investors to utilize this tool in ways that were once reserved for major financial institutions.

Today, leverage plays a key role in many financial markets, each with its unique dynamics and characteristics. In the Forex market, for instance, high leverage ratios such as 100:1 or more are common due to the highly liquid nature of the market and the relative stability of major currency pairs. This level of leverage allows traders to capitalize on small changes in exchange rates, turning them into significant profit opportunities, though it also entails a higher risk of substantial losses.

In the stock market, access to leverage is generally more moderate compared to Forex, primarily due to regulations aimed at protecting investors. By using margins, traders can increase their purchasing power and access broader investment opportunities. However, the risk associated with leveraging remains a critical consideration, as unfavorable market movements can quickly erode available capital.

Another area where leverage is widely used is in derivatives such as futures and options. These instruments allow traders to gain exposure to a wide range of assets with a relatively small initial investment, making them ideal for both speculative strategies and hedging purposes. However, their highly leveraged nature requires in-depth knowledge and careful planning to avoid incurring losses that are disproportionate to the initial capital.

The use of leverage demands a deep understanding of its mechanisms and strict discipline in risk management. Its amplifying nature makes it essential to carefully balance the ambition for profit with prudence. Responsible leverage management can turn it into an extraordinary tool for increasing returns, while an impulsive or unplanned approach can lead to disastrous consequences. Leverage, therefore, is not just an opportunity but also a responsibility. Traders must learn to use it wisely, understanding that long-term success in trading depends not only on the ability to seize opportunities but also on the wisdom to protect their capital.

How Financial Leverage Works

The operational mechanism of financial leverage in online trading allows traders to multiply their market exposure using only a fraction of the total value of the position they wish to control. This capability to amplify both potential profits and losses makes leverage a powerful yet risky tool. Understanding its dynamics involves delving into three essential components: the trader's initial capital, the borrowed funds, and the total size of the position.

At its core, leverage relies on a security deposit known as the margin. This initial amount is committed by the trader to open a leveraged position, serving as collateral for the broker to cover potential losses. The required margin percentage varies based on the broker, market conditions, and position size. For instance, a 1% margin requirement means that for every $100,000 invested, the trader needs to deposit $1,000 of their own funds.

The remainder of the position's value, exceeding the trader's margin, is provided by the broker as a form of loan. This borrowed capital enables traders to access significantly larger market positions than their initial investment. Rather than receiving physical funds, traders are granted the ability to control positions with amplified exposure, increasing both their profit potential and their risk of loss.

The total position size reflects the combined value of the trader's margin and the broker's loan. This amount determines the potential profit or loss, as any percentage change in the market's value affects the trader's capital proportionally to the leverage used. For example, with a leverage ratio of 10:1, a margin of $1,000 allows the trader to control a position worth $10,000, magnifying any market movements by the same factor.

To illustrate, imagine a trader investing in the Forex market. With a 2% margin requirement and a 50:1 leverage ratio, the trader can open a $100,000 position by depositing just $2,000. If the market moves favorably, the profits are calculated based on the $100,000 position, amplifying the return on investment. Conversely, if the market moves against the trader, losses accumulate rapidly, risking the initial margin and possibly requiring additional funds to maintain the position.

Understanding the interplay between the trader's capital, broker-provided leverage, and market dynamics is crucial for effective risk management. For instance, if a trader wishes to open a €10,000 position in the Forex market with 10:1 leverage, they would deposit €1,000 as margin, while the broker lends the remaining €9,000. This arrangement allows the trader to control a position much larger than their initial investment, amplifying both their opportunities and risks.

Practical Examples

In Forex trading, a trader might aim to speculate on the appreciation of the EUR against the USD. With a margin of €1,000 and leverage of 100:1, the trader can control a €100,000 position. If the EUR appreciates by 0.5% against the USD, the profit on the position would be €500, representing a 50% return on the initial investment. However, an equivalent adverse price movement would result in a €500 loss, highlighting the high risk associated with leverage.

In stock trading, consider a trader using 5:1 leverage to purchase shares of a specific company. With an investment of €2,000, the trader can control shares worth €10,000. If the share price increases by 10%, the profit would be €1,000 (10% of €10,000), doubling the initial investment. Conversely, a decrease in the share price would proportionally magnify the negative impact on the trader's capital.

Benefits

Leverage offers traders the opportunity to amplify potential profits significantly compared to what could be achieved using only their own capital. It also provides access to larger market positions, enabling better portfolio diversification even with limited capital.

Risks

The primary risk of leverage lies in the potential for losses to exceed the initial investment. Leverage magnifies not only potential gains but also the exposure to losses. Additionally, traders may face margin calls if the value of their positions moves against them. In such cases, brokers require additional deposits to maintain the position. Failing to meet a margin call can result in forced liquidation, locking in the losses.

Leverage Risks in Focus

Leverage is a double-edged sword: while it can enhance profits, it can also exacerbate losses. Traders must recognize that losses can exceed the initial invested capital. For instance, using 10:1 leverage on a €1,000 trade means a 1% adverse movement in the underlying asset results in a 10%

loss of the trader's capital. If the asset value drops by 10%, the entire capital is lost, and further losses may still accrue.

Adverse scenarios include the speed of losses, especially in highly volatile markets, where price changes can be rapid and substantial. Without stop-loss orders or other risk mitigation strategies, traders may incur significant losses within a short period. Margin calls also pose a challenge. If the value of held assets falls below a specific level, brokers may demand additional funds to maintain the positions. Failure to meet such demands can result in forced position closures, often at unfavorable times.

Setting stop-loss orders can help limit losses by automatically closing a position when the market reaches a specified price level. Education and practice are critical before employing leverage, with traders encouraged to practice in a risk-free demo account environment. Active monitoring of open positions is essential as market conditions can change rapidly. Maintaining a capital reserve provides a buffer for meeting margin calls without closing positions prematurely.

Margin and Margin Management

The margin is the capital required by an investor to open a leveraged position. It serves as collateral for the broker to cover the position's risk. A margin call occurs when a trader's account value falls below the broker's minimum required margin. In such cases, the trader must deposit additional funds to maintain their positions. Failure to do so may lead to the broker liquidating the positions to preserve their capital.

Effective margin management involves understanding broker policies regarding margin and margin calls, maintaining a margin level well above the required minimum to avoid margin calls, and using leverage cautiously. Traders should gradually increase leverage as they gain experience and confidence.

Responsible use of leverage requires a deep understanding of its associated risks. Traders must balance the aspiration to enhance profits with the necessity to protect their capital. Through education, prudent risk management, and strategic planning, traders can harness the benefits of leverage while minimizing the likelihood of uncontrolled losses.

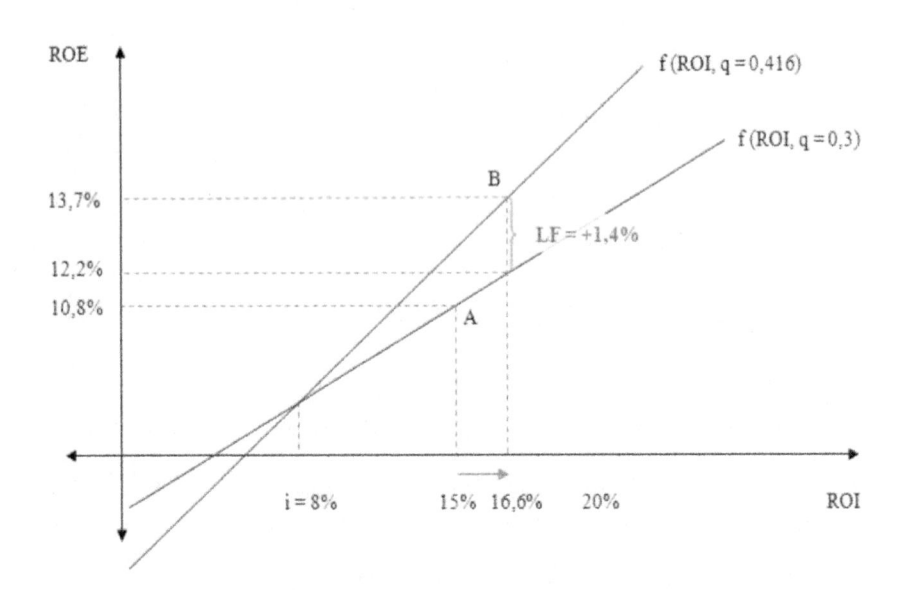

This type of chart, known as the "ROE (Return on Equity) versus ROI (Return on Investment) chart," is often used to illustrate how a company's ROE can be influenced by the use of financial leverage. ROI, or Return on Investment, is a key indicator of the profitability of an investment. It measures the return on an investment relative to its cost, providing a straightforward way to evaluate and compare different investment opportunities.

In the chart, the horizontal axis represents ROI, or return on investment, while the vertical axis indicates ROE, or return on equity. The lines demonstrate how ROE varies at different levels of ROI and degrees of financial leverage applied. The intersection between financial leverage and ROI highlights the effect leverage has on ROE.

Point A represents the ROE without the use of financial leverage, while point B shows the ROE achieved with leverage. The vertical distance between the two points reflects the percentage increase in ROE resulting from the application of leverage. This distinction is critical for understanding the positive impact that well-managed leverage can have on equity returns.

In an educational context, the chart is particularly valuable for demonstrating how positive financial leverage can enhance ROE when ROI exceeds the interest rate on debt. However, it also highlights the associated risks. A drop in ROI below the interest rate on debt can not only decrease ROE but also significantly increase a company's financial vulnerability. This duality underscores the importance of using financial leverage thoughtfully and strategically to optimize returns while minimizing risks.

Leverage	Calculation	Margin
1:10	100/10 =	10%
1:50	100/50 =	2%
1:100	100/100 =	1%
1:200	100/200 =	0.5%
1:500	100/500 =	0.2%

The table above illustrates the direct relationship between leverage and the required margin, providing a clear overview of how leverage levels impact the amount of own capital needed to open a position in the market. This representation is particularly useful for understanding the importance of margin and the potential risks associated with using leverage.

In trading, leverage is expressed as a ratio, such as 1:10 or 1:500, indicating the market exposure allowed relative to the trader's deposited capital. The margin column shows the percentage of the total position value that the trader must provide as an initial deposit.

For example:

- With leverage of 1:10, the required margin is 10%. This means that to control a position worth $10,000, the trader must deposit $1,000 as margin.

- With leverage of 1:500, the required margin decreases to 0.2%. In this case, to control a position of the same value, the trader would only need to deposit $20.

This table demonstrates two key aspects:

1. **Higher leverage, lower required margin:** As leverage increases, traders can open larger positions using a smaller amount of their own capital. However, this also amplifies both potential gains and losses.

2. **Importance of risk control:** With higher leverage, even small market movements can significantly impact the trader's account. This makes it essential to use risk management strategies, such as stop-loss orders and limiting overall exposure.

The table also highlights how critical it is to fully understand the concept of leverage before utilizing it in trading. For beginners, it is advisable to start with lower leverage levels, gradually increasing as they gain more experience and confidence in their trading methods.

Leverage is undoubtedly one of the most powerful tools available to traders, capable of amplifying both earning opportunities and the risks of loss. The key to leveraging it successfully lies in a deep understanding of its mechanics and the adoption of rigorous risk management practices. For traders, leverage offers a unique opportunity to access markets and positions that would otherwise be out of reach, but it demands discipline, education, and a clear strategy to avoid costly mistakes. With a mindful and well-planned approach, leverage can become a valuable ally in achieving financial goals.

Chapter 10: The Psychology of Trading

In the vibrant and often unforgiving world of trading, charts, algorithms, and strategies might appear to be the undisputed protagonists. However, beneath the surface of every market tick and behind every opened or closed position lies a fundamental yet invisible element: the trader's psychology. This chapter delves into the depths of a trader's mind, exploring the darker corners where greed and fear reside, as well as the radiant light of discipline and rationality.

Trading psychology is the minefield through which every investor must navigate. Understanding how greed can turn an opportunity into a disastrous loss or how fear can paralyze and prevent crucial moments from being seized is vital for long-term success. However, it is not only the awareness of these emotions that is essential but also the development of tools to manage them. This chapter not only identifies and dissects these emotions but also provides strategies for forging the discipline and rational approach necessary to navigate the turbulent waters of financial markets.

Through real-life anecdotes, in-depth research, and practical advice, we aim to build a trader who rises above emotional storms, someone with the clarity and control to excel in the relentless chaos of trading. Prepare to embark on a transformative journey, one that promises to strengthen not only your trading decisions but also your personal and professional resilience.

Understanding Greed, Fear, and the Impact of Emotions on Trading Decisions

Trading is an activity that can be both profitable and risky, and emotions often influence a trader's ability to act logically and consistently. Greed and fear are two of the most influential emotions in trading and can lead to impulsive decisions that deviate from a well-thought-out trading plan.

Greed represents the excessive desire for greater financial gains, often beyond what is reasonably achievable or prudent. In trading, greed manifests in various ways, including overtrading, neglecting sound money management principles, or failing to lock in profits due to the hope of even greater gains. Fear, on the other hand, reflects the anxiety or expectation of loss. It can be equally detrimental, leading to panic selling, hesitation in executing trades, or avoiding the market altogether due to negative past experiences or a heightened aversion to risk.

The emotional impact on trading decisions is not limited to individual moments of greed or fear but often results in a broader pattern of impulsive actions, confirmation bias, or overconfidence following temporary success. Managing these impulses is essential for becoming a successful trader. Self-control and discipline are not just desirable traits but fundamental requirements for those who wish to operate effectively in financial markets.

Developing Discipline and a Rational Approach to Trading

Developing discipline and a rational approach to trading is not merely about adhering to a set of rules; it is a deeply personal journey that involves introspection, self-awareness, and acknowledgment of one's limits. At the heart of this process is the recognition that trading is not just an intellectual challenge but also an intensely emotional experience.

Trading discipline is often compared to the discipline required in high-level sports. Like athletes, traders must train, stay focused on their goals, and resist distractions and pressures that could derail them. However, unlike athletes, traders often work in isolation, without the direct support of a team or coach. This makes discipline even more challenging, requiring constant self-motivation and self-regulation.

One of the most human aspects of trading is how losses are handled. Losses and gains provide the most immediate and tangible feedback from the market, and the way traders react to them can define their long-term success. Developing a rational approach requires mastering the art of accepting losses as part of the trading process. Losses should not be viewed as personal failures but as opportunities to learn and refine strategies.

Greed, too, is a powerful force that can drive traders to take excessive risks or hold onto profitable positions for too long in the hope of earning even more. Combating greed requires ongoing self-control and the ability to adhere to a trading plan, even when every fiber of one's being wants to defy established rules.

Discipline also involves managing time and energy effectively. Trading can be exhausting, and burnout is a real risk. Recognizing signs of fatigue and stress and taking breaks when necessary is crucial for maintaining a clear mind and consistent decision-making.

A rational approach to trading thrives on the support of a community or mentor. Sharing experiences with other traders, learning from their successes and failures, and receiving sound advice from those who have already walked the path can be immensely beneficial. External support can help mitigate the isolation that often accompanies trading and provide a vital sense of perspective.

In conclusion, while trading techniques and tools can be learned, discipline and a rational approach are qualities developed through time and experience. They are the result of a personal commitment to continuous improvement and a balance between mind, emotions, and actions. Every trader embarks on a unique journey, and the ability to navigate the human aspect of trading ultimately distinguishes great traders from mere market participants.

Chapter 11: Developing a Trading Plan

Building a trading plan is one of the cornerstones of a trader's career. It is the manifesto that defines not only strategies but also the mental approach, expectations, and individual goals. In Chapter 11, we dive into the core of the trading process, exploring the fundamental importance of having a well-articulated trading plan.

A trading strategy serves as your beacon in the storm of financial markets. It guides you through the turbulent waters of volatility and uncertainty. Beyond being a map to navigate the markets, it is also an emotional control system, helping you stay anchored to your principles when the waves of fear and greed threaten to sweep you away.

Developing and testing a trading strategy is not merely a technical exercise; it is a process of self-discovery and personal growth. As you refine your strategy, you will also uncover your limits, behavioral tendencies, and psychological predispositions. This journey goes far beyond mere technical or fundamental analysis; it is a path of both professional and personal development.

A trading journal acts as your faithful chronicler, a companion that allows you to track your progress and learn from your mistakes. Through this reflective practice, trading evolves from an intuition-based activity into a discipline grounded in concrete data, learned lessons, and refined strategies.

This chapter focuses on understanding the intrinsic value of a trading plan, how to create a personalized one that reflects your unique circumstances and objectives, and how self-analysis through a trading journal can be the key to continuous growth and improvement in the trading world.

The Importance of Having a Trading Plan

The importance of a trading plan can be compared to the necessity of a map when traveling through uncharted territory. Trading in financial markets, with its inherent complexity and unpredictable fluctuations, requires a compass to guide traders toward well-thought-out, strategically sound decisions. Without a plan, traders rely on chance and emotion, two elements often synonymous with long-term failure.

A trading plan provides a structured framework for your investments, offering a set of guidelines to help you make informed and consistent decisions. This vital document should detail your entry and exit strategies, risk and reward parameters, money management techniques, and criteria for performance evaluation. It enables disciplined operation, preventing emotions like fear and greed from taking over.

Setting clear goals is one of the key aspects of a trading plan. It compels you to define short- and long-term financial and personal objectives. These goals should be SMART: Specific, Measurable, Achievable, Realistic, and Time-bound. With clear objectives, you can measure success and make targeted adjustments along the way.

Managing risk is another essential component of a trading plan. It helps you establish acceptable loss limits for both individual positions and your entire portfolio. Defining in advance how much you are willing to lose in a single trade aids in risk management and protects your capital.

Consistency is fundamental for long-term success in trading. A trading plan ensures that all trades are executed in alignment with a well-thought-out strategy, reducing the likelihood of impulsive and inconsistent decisions.

Finally, evaluation and revision are crucial. A trading plan is not a static document; it is a living guide that should be reviewed and adapted as markets evolve and you grow as a trader. Periodic performance evaluations based on the plan can reveal strengths to capitalize on and weaknesses to improve.

A trading plan acts as a beacon of rationality in an environment characterized by uncertainty. It is the foundation upon which a sustainable trading career is built, allowing you to move forward with confidence and clarity, knowing that every decision is the result of a well-considered process rather than chance or emotional impulse.

How to Develop and Test a Trading Strategy

Developing and testing a trading strategy are critical steps to ensure the robustness and effectiveness of your approach to the market. This process requires research, analysis, and systematic experimentation.

Start by defining your objectives. Clearly outline what you aim to achieve through trading, including your desired return on investment, acceptable risk levels, time availability, and preferred trading style (day trading, swing trading, position trading, etc.).

Next, select the market and instruments that align with your objectives. Assess various asset classes such as stocks, bonds, currencies, and commodities, and decide where to focus based on volatility, liquidity, and your expertise.

Define clear entry and exit criteria. These can be based on technical or fundamental analysis, market events, or a combination of factors. Identify signals that indicate when to open or close a position.

Risk management is a cornerstone of any trading strategy. Establish guidelines for position sizing, the use of stop-loss and take-profit levels, and rules for diversification and correlation among different positions.

Once your strategy is defined, backtesting is essential. Using historical data, simulate how your strategy would have performed in the past. Backtesting provides insights into how your strategy might react to various market conditions and helps refine it before testing with real capital.

Before committing actual funds, practice your strategy in real-time without risking money. Many brokers offer trading simulators that allow you to engage in virtual trading with live market data. This step is vital for assessing the feasibility of your strategy and familiarizing yourself with order execution mechanisms.

After testing, analyze the results of your backtesting and simulated trading. Examine metrics such as the percentage of winning trades, risk/reward ratio, maximum drawdown, and other performance parameters. Adjust your strategy based on the insights gained.

When you feel confident in your strategy and have observed positive results in testing, begin trading with a small amount of real capital. Monitor performance continuously and be prepared to make adjustments if the strategy fails to deliver the expected outcomes.

Lastly, keep in mind that markets are dynamic and constantly changing. A strategy effective today might not be tomorrow. Regularly review and update your strategy to ensure it remains aligned with current market conditions and your evolving goals.

Keeping a Trading Journal to Monitor Progress and Mistakes

A detailed trading journal should include basic information about each trade, such as date, time, asset, entry and exit prices, position size, and realized profits or losses. This helps you track the effectiveness of your strategies and your ability to execute them correctly.

In addition to quantitative data, record the reasons behind each trading decision, including market analysis, economic news, or technical indicators that influenced your choice. This provides context for your trades and allows you to evaluate the soundness of your decision-making strategies.

Over time, analyzing your journal entries can reveal recurring patterns in both successful and unsuccessful trades. You might discover that certain approaches work better in specific market conditions or that some mistakes are repeated frequently. This awareness can guide you in optimizing your strategy.

Incorporating a trading journal into your routine can become one of the most valuable investments in your development as a trader. It offers a detailed map of your progress and areas for improvement, fostering continuous learning and refinement in your trading journey.

Chapter 12: Technological Innovation in Trading

Technological evolution in trading has been nothing short of a revolution, bringing profound changes to how individuals and institutions access and participate in global financial markets. This transformation has reshaped interactions with the stock market and Forex, democratizing investment access and providing advanced tools for analysis and decision-making.

At the end of the 20th century, the advent of online trading marked the beginning of this evolution, shifting activities from bustling trading floors and telephone-placed orders to digital platforms enabling global market operations with just a click. This transition ushered in an era of unprecedented accessibility, effectively removing geographical barriers to investment.

With the emergence of mobile apps, advanced AI-driven analysis, machine learning, and high-frequency trading algorithms, technology has continued to advance, enabling transactions in fractions of a second and providing traders with increasingly sophisticated tools for market analysis and investment management.

This rapid evolution has significantly impacted stock and Forex trading, offering numerous benefits. Access to financial markets has become more inclusive, allowing anyone with an internet connection to participate actively in trading. Operational speed and efficiency have skyrocketed, improving the effectiveness of trading and making real-time market information indispensable, particularly in the dynamic Forex environment.

Market analysis tools, enriched by AI capabilities, have revolutionized how traders interpret data, enabling more accurate analyses and reliable market movement predictions. Automation in trading, using algorithms and bots, has allowed for complex strategies to be executed precisely without constant human intervention, minimizing the emotional influence on trading decisions.

Technology has also significantly enhanced access to educational resources and training tools, facilitating the efficient development and refinement of trading skills. In essence, technological innovation in trading has simplified and streamlined access to stock and Forex markets while opening new possibilities for analysis, decision-making, and automation. As technology progresses, we can expect further advancements that will continue to reshape financial markets and the strategies traders adopt to navigate them.

The Online Trading Platform Revolution

The online trading platform revolution stands as one of the most significant changes in the trading world over the past few decades. This transformation began in the 1990s when the internet became widely accessible, paving the way for the development of the first online trading platforms. These initial systems marked the beginning of a new era, enabling individual investors to access financial markets directly from their home computers.

The history of online trading platforms is closely linked to the evolution of the internet and information technologies. In their early days, these platforms were rudimentary, offering limited functionality and user-unfriendly interfaces. However, their potential to democratize investment access was evident. As technology advanced, platforms became more sophisticated, integrating advanced analytical tools, real-time charts, updated financial news, and near-instant order execution.

The contrast between traditional trading and online trading is stark. Traditionally, investors relied on brokers to execute trades, often through phone calls, which made the process slow and occasionally inefficient. Additionally, access to market information was limited and often delayed. With the rise of online trading, investors gained direct control over their operations, with real-time access to market data and analysis, enabling them to make informed decisions independently.

Benefits of Online Trading Platforms: Accessibility and Efficiency

Online trading platforms have revolutionized how individuals access financial markets, offering numerous advantages:

Accessibility: Anyone with an internet connection can now participate in trading without the need for intermediaries. This has broken down geographical and social barriers, significantly expanding the pool of investors. Efficiency: Transactions can be executed within seconds, allowing traders to capitalize on market opportunities as they arise. This speed is crucial in volatile markets like Forex. Reduced Costs: The elimination of intermediaries and competition among platforms have lowered commissions, making online trading economically advantageous. Advanced Tools: Platforms offer technical and fundamental analysis tools, charts, trading signals, and more, enabling traders to develop sophisticated strategies based on accurate, up-to-date data. Education and Training: Many platforms provide educational resources, webinars, tutorials, and demo accounts, facilitating learning and trading practice without risk.

Artificial Intelligence and Machine Learning in Trading

The advent of Artificial Intelligence (AI) and Machine Learning (ML) in trading has ushered in an era of radical change, redefining how market participants analyze data, make decisions, and manage operations. These technologies, with their ability to process and learn from vast datasets in real time, provide unprecedented tools for identifying trends, predicting market movements, and optimizing strategies.

AI enables predictive analysis at a level of detail and accuracy unimaginable with traditional methods. Advanced systems now sift through the vast data generated by financial markets—including economic indicators, corporate reports, price data, and even social media sentiment—to identify investment opportunities or warning signs that might elude human analysis.

AI's ability to gauge market sentiment through extensive online content analysis, such as social media posts and news articles, offers traders valuable insights into potential market directions. Similarly, AI-driven risk management identifies and mitigates potential risks, optimizing investment strategies for maximum returns while minimizing losses.

Despite its promise, the growing reliance on AI in trading is not without challenges. The complexity of ML algorithms can make it difficult to understand the rationale behind specific trading decisions, raising transparency and trust issues. Over-optimization is another risk, where models fine-tuned to historical data may falter under unforeseen market conditions.

Moreover, AI's ability to execute trades at unmatched speed and volume raises concerns about market volatility and stability. Algorithms reacting almost instantaneously to changes could, in theory, amplify market fluctuations, leading to extreme price movements. Ethical and security concerns also loom large, especially regarding data management and protection. Cybersecurity and data privacy are paramount in an increasingly digitalized world, particularly when handling sensitive financial information.

Blockchain and Cryptocurrencies: A New Paradigm

The introduction of blockchain technology and the rise of cryptocurrencies represent some of the most transformative innovations in the financial landscape over the past decades. These advancements have not only introduced new financial instruments but also laid the groundwork for a new paradigm of security, transparency, and decentralization in financial markets.

Blockchain technology, with its unique, immutable data structure, provides a new avenue for securely recording and transmitting financial information, eliminating the need for traditional intermediaries like banks. This potential to significantly reduce transaction costs and times, while offering unparalleled security and transparency, has reshaped the concept of financial transactions.

Cryptocurrencies have emerged as a new asset class, combining the properties of digital currency with those of an investment vehicle. Their decentralized nature challenges traditional financial control mechanisms, offering unprecedented opportunities for financial inclusion. Yet, they also bring security, volatility, and regulatory challenges that require careful navigation.

Automation, Big Data Analysis, and Online Security

The digital era has brought radical changes to trading methodologies, such as employing trading robots, leveraging Big Data analysis, and prioritizing online security. These innovations have transformed how investments are managed, presenting opportunities and challenges.

Automated trading systems, Big Data-driven strategies, and robust cybersecurity measures now define the landscape of modern trading. Together, they underscore the importance of balancing technological advantages with prudent trading practices to succeed in this dynamic environment.

Technological advancements, such as AI, quantum computing, and enhanced blockchain networks, promise to further transform trading. The future lies in integrating these innovations responsibly to ensure that traders can leverage new opportunities while managing emerging risks effectively.

Chapter 13: Fundamental Trading Terminologies

1. **Stock:** A security representing ownership in a corporation and a claim on part of its assets and earnings.

2. **Bond:** A debt security issued by a corporation or government, which pays fixed interest over a specific period.

3. **Forex (FX):** The global market for exchanging national currencies.

4. **Cryptocurrency:** A digital currency used for online transactions and investments.

5. **Futures:** A standardized contract to buy or sell an asset at a predetermined price on a future date.

6. **Option:** A financial contract granting the right, but not the obligation, to buy or sell an asset at a specified price by a certain date.

7. **ETF (Exchange-Traded Fund):** A fund that tracks an index, commodity, bonds, or a basket of assets like an index fund, but trades on a stock exchange like a stock.

8. **Leverage:** The use of borrowed capital to increase the potential return on an investment.

9. **Margin:** The amount of capital required in a trading account to open a leveraged position.

10. **Stop Loss:** An order to sell an asset when it reaches a specified price, used to limit losses.

11. **Take Profit:** An order to sell an asset when it reaches a target price, used to secure profits.

12. **Technical Analysis:** The study of price charts and trading volumes to predict future price movements.

13. **Fundamental Analysis:** The evaluation of assets based on economic, financial, and other qualitative and quantitative factors.

14. **Spread:** The difference between the ask (buy) price and the bid (sell) price of an asset.

15. **Volatility:** A measure of how much an asset's price fluctuates over time; high volatility indicates significant price swings.

16. **Liquidity:** The ease with which an asset can be bought or sold in the market without affecting its price.

17. **Bull Market:** Market conditions characterized by rising prices.

18. **Bear Market:** Market conditions characterized by falling prices.

19. **Diversification:** An investment strategy that involves holding a variety of assets to reduce risk.

20. **Market Risk:** The risk of an investment losing value due to changes in market conditions.

These terms are just a glimpse of the foundational language used in trading. Building a solid understanding of these and other terminologies is crucial as you deepen your knowledge of trading and refine your investment strategies. Whether you're a beginner or an experienced trader, staying informed and continually expanding your vocabulary will enhance your ability to navigate the complexities of financial markets effectively.

As markets evolve, so too does the language used to describe them. Keeping up with the latest terminologies and concepts ensures that you remain agile and well-prepared to adapt to new opportunities and challenges. Trading is as much about understanding the tools and principles as it is about mastering the language that underpins this dynamic field.

Conclusion

This guide has been a journey through the fundamentals of online trading, exploring its dynamics, the key tools available, and the essential strategies to effectively navigate financial markets. From understanding the basics and history of trading to delving into the technological innovations reshaping the industry, each chapter has been designed to provide a solid foundation of knowledge, valuable for both beginners and seasoned traders.

We have examined the core principles of financial markets, from the stock market to Forex, cryptocurrencies, and derivatives. We discussed the importance of risk management, the necessity of a structured trading plan, and the role of discipline in navigating the highs and lows of market fluctuations. The section on trading psychology highlighted how mental balance is as crucial as technical skills, while the analysis of technological innovations, such as artificial intelligence and blockchain, offered insights into future possibilities and the tools already available to enhance performance.

This guide represents only the beginning of a continuous learning journey. Trading is a dynamic activity that constantly evolves, and maintaining an open and adaptive mindset is essential for success. Every reader is encouraged to view this book not as an endpoint but as a springboard toward a deeper understanding and growing mastery of the techniques and strategies needed.

Continuing to invest in personal education is the key to success. Whether through advanced courses, seminars, or regular practice with demo accounts, every effort to hone skills builds the confidence and expertise necessary to trade successfully. Sharing experiences with other traders, analyzing results through a trading journal, and engaging with industry experts are additional tools that can accelerate growth and expand perspectives.

Success in trading is never the result of a magical formula or standardized approach; instead, it stems from consistent effort, discipline, and the willingness to learn from mistakes. This guide has provided the foundation for beginning the journey, but your success will depend on your dedication and desire for continuous improvement.

With the knowledge gained, you are now better equipped to face challenges and seize opportunities in financial markets. Whether you are starting your journey or refining established strategies, remember that every step forward is a step closer to achieving your goals.

The future of trading is full of possibilities—explore it with awareness, passion, and a clear vision. With the right balance of learning, practice, and perseverance, you will be ready to tackle challenges and leverage opportunities in this fascinating world.

Expand Your Knowledge with Bonus Chapters

If you're interested in diving deeper into the world of trading and exploring topics such as **options trading** and **stock trading,** we have prepared two bonus chapters dedicated to these essential areas. These additional materials will help you understand the principles of how options work, key strategies like calls and puts, and the dynamics of stock trading, focusing on analytical techniques and practical approaches.

To access these bonus chapters, simply use the QR code below. Download the PDF and discover everything you need to know to further expand your understanding of trading. This is an opportunity to delve into strategic topics and enhance your skills wherever you are.

Printed in Dunstable, United Kingdom